Financial Stability Series

I0483845

How to Build Credit

How to Improve Your Credit Score & Rebuild Credit

By

Kimberly Peters

Also Available in the
Financial Fitness Series:

How to Retire Happy
& Financially Secure

For more titles on other
subjects, please visit our
website at:

http://www.26ways.com

Contents

Disclaimer

This publication is intended to be used as an educational resource only. It is not intended to be used as a specific action plan or financial plan for any one specific individual. Everyone one is different and everyone's situation is different as well. Because of this there is no one all-purpose approach to credit building or financial security. In addition, because there is no one perfect approach, some or all parts of this book may or may not be appropriate for any specific situation or person. Because of this, the reader assumes full responsibility for determining which parts of this publication are appropriate for their situation. The writers, publishers and resellers of this publication assume no responsibility for the application or suitability of any or all parts of this book.

Introduction

For most of us credit is a way of life. It is how we pay for our purchases so we don't have to carry around large sums of money or constantly go to the bank. It is how we pay for online purchases quickly and easily so we don't have to bother writing checks and delaying shipment. We also use our credit cards as proof of identification. Just try renting a car without a credit card and see how far you get.

In other words, credit has become a vital part of our lives and it has become very difficult, if not impossible, to lead a normal life without owning, and regularly using a credit card. This is no longer the world that your father and his father used to live in. We are a credit card based world now and you cannot escape it.

We also use credit to be able to purchase the things we really need in life but cannot expect to pay for in cash.

Houses, automobiles, college or higher education are just a few things that we regularly pay for with credit of some kind.

After all, few people have $250,000 in cash to purchase their first home or $150,000 to pay for their college education. On a smaller scale, many people do not have the $20,000 necessary to purchase a new car either.

For those purchases, credit is a necessity and not just something that makes purchasing convenient. In those cases, credit makes us able to get what we need in life much easier and faster than if we had to rely on others or wait until we had saved up what we needed to buy what we wanted.

But even though credit has made life much easier for many people, it has also made life a lot more difficult for others. That is because some people abused their credit or let their spending get away from them because it was so convenient to get what they wanted when they wanted it. In fact, credit has enable our culture to become a lot more entitled than previous generation ever were.

When your grandfather wanted something, he either had to go to the bank and take out a loan or pay for it by cash or check. Both those latter options required that you had money is the bank in order to purchase something. If you didn't have the money, you didn't make the purchase. This was kind of a forced budget for many people.

But today, if you want something, you swipe the card or hit the home equity loan.

You want it, you but it, you enjoy it and then you almost faint when the bill comes at the end of the month. But wait! It's not so bad! You might owe $4,500 but you only have to pay $50.00 because that is the minimum payment! So it's not a big deal, right.

Except for the 18% interest.

Credit card debt is one of the easiest to accrue and one of the most expensive to pay off. Credit card rates remain sky high and the worse your credit rating is the higher interest you pay! Some people never get out of debt because of the high interest payments they have to pay every month.

The credit companies don't mind because they are making a HUGE return on their investment. I mean, if you could get 18% on your money wouldn't you be happy? Even if they have to write off some bad debts once in a while they are still making a killing! So the credit card companies are not your friend for letting you have one of their cards, you are their income source!

So this leads us to trying to decide how we can live a normal life with credit even if we might have made a few mistakes or are just trying to start out in life and establish some credit history.

Fortunately there are easy things anyone can do to help themselves establish good credit, repair some bad credit and even start over if they found themselves with really bad credit because of some past mistakes.

Make no mistake about it, you CAN do this! In fact, you really have no choice if you want to live even a reasonable happy and successful life. You need credit to live although not to the extent most people seem to think they do. But you can use credit to your advantage and you can come out on top after everything is said and done.

We are here to show you how to accomplish all of this and more. All you have to do is sit back and read this book and follow the tips and techniques we give you to create a solid credit score or recover from past mistakes.

You CAN do this, you NEED to do this and we are going to show you HOW to do this!

Let's get started!

Part One:
Credit Basics & Attitudes

Things you should know to help you move forward and get back on the right track!

What is a Credit Score?

A credit score is usually a 3 digit number that is calculated by lenders to rank your suitability for credit and your overall credit worthiness. The higher your score the better your overall risk is considered to be. This score will be used throughout your life to determine whether or not you get approved for a credit card or loan and at what interest rate. So this is something you need to be aware of and take seriously.

There are several factors that are taken into consideration by the three major credit reporting agencies. These may include your open credit accounts, amount of outstanding credit, your payment history, your past performance in paying back loans and outstanding balances and several other factors. Each reporting agency may use slightly different methods of arriving at your credit score.

Your credit report will consist of everything that happens with your credit history. Every inquiry, every payment, every request for credit will be noted. These will either be positive entries and will raise your credit score or negative things that will lower it. Naturally the more positive things the better and the fewer negative things the better as well. Simple said, your credit rating is a snapshot of how well and responsibly you use credit in your life.

This is why it is important to get all three of your credit reports. Since some information may only show up on one or two of your reports, it is critical that you examine all 3 to make sure they are 100% accurate and correct. If there are false or unknown entries on your report you need to check them out so your credit rating accurately reflects you and how you use credit.

These agencies do not produce the information they use they gather it from the companies that you have credit accounts with. That means your credit card companies, retailer charge accounts, gas cards, bank loans or any other kind of credit is reported to these agencies so that everyone will have an accurate picture of what kind of person you are from a credit standpoint.

Though it might not be fair or seem fair, companies will draw certain conclusions about you based on your credit score.

Credit card companies will think people with higher scores are more responsible because they have shown this by paying off their bills and making payments on time. A poor credit rating might make companies feel that you are not responsible and are therefore a poor risk. In other words, sometimes it makes little difference WHY your credit rating is low. All that matters is that it is low.

For this reason, it is very important that we treat credit, and our credit score very, very seriously. Some entries on our credit report can stay on that report for 10 years so what we do today can very well impact us 5 or 8 years from now! So if we are considering buying a house in 5 years, the mortgage rate we get, if we get approved at all, may depend on what we do with our credit today.

If you are thinking about doing anything today that will cause you to get in over your head when it comes to credit or if you are thinking about missing a credit card payment so you can go away for the weekend with friends instead, I seriously suggest you stop and reconsider. Because like we said, what you do today is going to stick with you for several years to come.

What is a Good Credit Score?

Now that we understand what a credit rating really is, the next question is what is considered a good credit rating? Does it need to be perfect? How is my credit rating or credit score going to impact me when I apply for credit in the future? The more common question is often just "How am I doing so far when it comes to credit?"

The following is a very rough explanation of what good, decent and poor scores might represent. Keep in mind that these are only approximations and these can vary over time as the financial institutions change their requirements when it comes to credit.

751++   top notch qualify at lowest rates

711-750   you will qualify for most credit at competitive rates

651-710   you may qualify at moderate rates

581 – 650   may or may not qualify at
higher rates

300-580 will be denied or only given the
highest rates

So if you had a credit rating of 775 and
you applied for a loan, you would likely get
that loan at one of the lowest interest rates.
That is because you would be considered an
excellent credit risk. That means you are
someone who uses credit responsibly and has
shown a history of paying their bills on time
and without problems. People at this level are
those most sought after by lenders.

If you had a credit rating of 725 and you
applied for a loan you would also likely be
approved at one of the lowest rates but
maybe not the absolute lowest. But a rating
this high still suggests that you are
responsible for credit and therefore are a
good risk for credit. People at this level are
sought after as well.

If you had a rating of 675, however, this
is the start of the levels where lenders might
have questions about your ability to handle
credit responsibly. This means you might still
get approved but the lender will probably
demand a higher interest rate because of the
increased possibility of late payments or
default.

If you were even lower at 625, you might be declined or, if you were approved you would pay a much higher interest rate because you had not demonstrated the ability to use credit responsibly. At this level, you would stand a pretty good chance of getting turned down especially for higher amounts of credit. By that I means for mortgages or auto loans. If you do get approved you would be paying very high interest rates.

If you are below 500 then you would be hard pressed to get approved for any decent loan. Instead you might have to take out a secured credit card or pay really, really high interest rates. People at this level strangely enough are usually the targets or credit offer for cards with astronomically high interest rates. For example, if the standard credit card rate for someone with a 750 credit rating was 12%, a person with a rating of 450 might be paying 28% or higher!

That is why it is so important to keep your credit score as high as possible and to rebuild your credit if it should fall for some reason. Life is full or unexpected situations and sometimes things happen and we fall off our payments a bit. It happens. But when that happens we need to take certain actions and make certain adjustments to minimize the damage and to get on with recovery and rebuilding as soon as possible.

It's All about Future Risk

When it comes to our credit rating, lender subscribe to a simple premise. That is that what we have done in the past is a very good indicator of what we are going to do in the future. So if we were good with credit in the past, we are likely to be good with it in the future as well. But if we were bad with credit in the past, we had better show improvement or we might never get credit again.

You see, lenders don't know us personally. Because of this they do not have any idea what kind of person we are or what kind of risk we might be. So they use our credit scores to determine who has what level of risk. The lower the overall risk, the more likely it will be that we get approved at the lowest possible rate.

But if the lender sees a lower credit score they will make the assumption that you represent a higher risk in the future.

Whenever there is a higher risk, the interest rates go up. That means if you want to borrow money or establish a credit line, you will pay more for it than people with excellent credit.

Therefore, we need to do our best to show a long-standing ability to use credit responsibly.

That is one reason why our credit scores are determined by several years' worth of data and activity. We cannot take a bad credit rating and turn it into a great one by making next month's payments on time. We need to establish a long running pattern of good credit behavior and not just a month or two of paying on time.

Once you look at things from a creditor's point of view it makes it easier to understand what they are looking at and why such things are important to them. It's nothing personal between you and the lender. All things being equal they would love to lend you money because the more they lend the more interest they collect. But they want to make good investments that minimize their risk and exposure in the future.

Does This

"Interest" You?

When it comes to credit, one very important thing should really interest you. That one thing is the interest rate that you pay for the ability to pay for things on credit. Your focus should always be on paying the lowest rate on any kind of funds you access through credit.

Think about this for a minute:

If you walked into a store and the salesman told you that all prices were 18% higher today, would you buy or walk out? Unless what you needed was an absolute necessity, most people would probably walk out the door and wait for the prices to come back down to their normal levels.

What if you had to pay that additional 18% only if you paid for that item with your charge card? Would you still pay by charge or would you go to the bank and take out the cash so you could avoid the 18% surcharge?

With either of those examples, you would pay 18% more for whatever you bought if you used credit. But when you think about it, whenever you carry a balance on your charge card, or whenever you have an 18% loan to pay off, you are in fact paying 18% more for everything you purchase on that card!

No actually that 18% is over a full year so you are actually paying 1.5% per month but that is still money you have to pay someone just for the privilege of using their money. You don't get anything more for that extra charge other than being able to buy whatever you bought earlier and more conveniently than if you paid cash.

So if you bought a $100 product on your charge card at 18% and took a year to pay it off that product really costs you $118 not $100. So you spent another $18 for nothing. That $18 could have bought you a meal or two worth of food at the supermarket or dry cleaned some clothes. You could have seen a movie with a large popcorn as well in some areas. In other words, you would have actually received something for that $18 instead of just handing it over to someone else for nothing in return.

Now $18 might not seem like a lot of money but if you purchased $1,000 of something instead of just $100, than you would be paying $180 over the year for just using credit and that IS serious money! The more you pay for on your credit account or place on your outstanding loan balances, the more money you are paying and not receiving anything in return!

But we also understand that sometimes we must charge things either because they are just too expensive to be able to save up for and pay cash for or personal situations require that credit be used as a temporary or stop gap measure. We all have times in our lives when too many expenses come up at one time and therefore we have no choice but to take advantage of credit to help us continue to function.

So when it comes to using credit, we need to use it wisely and choose our credit c=sources wisely as well. Because if we choose the credit sources with the lowest interest rates, we can save more money and have more money left over to either pay down our outstanding balances or purchase additional things for cash instead of credit next month.

Using a very simple example, if we maintain a $1,000 balance on a credit card with an 18% interest rate that means we will be paying $180 for that privilege. But if we used a card with just a 12% rate, we would be paying just $120 and that would be a savings of $60 without sacrificing anything. If we rolled over the balance to a personal loan or home equity loan of 8% then we would save even more!

Let's say we use lower interest rate credit sources and manage to save just $50 a month in interest.

That is a savings of $600 a year which can be used to purchase more items for cash OR that might mean you would have $600 more during the year to pay down your outstanding balance! That translates into more savings because the lower your balance the less you pay in interest. So with lower interest credit you can pay off your balances faster with less sacrifice or struggle!

The point we are trying to make is that we should become very aware of interest rates because they can make using credit much easier and less costly if we manage the interest. There are a few ways we can manage the interest we pay on our credit cards and loans so that we can minimize costs.

Boost Your Credit Score

The higher your credit score, the better credit offers you will qualify for. That means lower interest credit cards, reductions in interest in your current cards and overall better control over what options are available to you when it comes to credit.

So don't think of creating a good credit history as something that helps you today but as also something that will help you get better and cheaper credit in the future as well. That can make the sacrifice easier to take and give you some additional motivation.

Shop Around for Lower Interest

If your credit score allows, consider checking the market for cards with lower interest rates. This is especially important if your credit scores were previously poor and you were forced to get one of those very high interest credit cards. If you have improved your credit history and credit score, you could be eligible for a new card with less interest.

In some cases people were able to take a high risk card, with interest rates approaching 30% and transfer balances to new cards with 15-18% interest rates sometimes lower! Since paying off balances with 30& interest rates is extremely difficult, it is always a good idea to see if there is anything you can do to qualify for lower interest rates.

Talk to your Lender or your Credit Card Company

I'm not saying this will work but if you have improved your credit score to the point where you would be eligible for lower interest rate cards, it might be worth the time to call your current company and ask them to consider reducing your rates. They might feel that it is better to give you a lower rate and keep your business rather than losing it all to another credit company.

This would only work if you can qualify for a better rate and only if you have improved your credit history and score.

Remember this is all about creditor risk so if you credit score is still at rock bottom, you are not likely to have the give you any break on interest rates. Why? Because you have not done anything to deserve reconsideration.

Personal Loans

If you can qualify, a personal loan usually will have lower interest rates which means you might have more money left over to pay down the balances because you had to pay less interest. But this approach will only work if you don't build up new credit card balances after you transfer you old credit card balances to your personal loan. Otherwise you will be paying off the personal load balance AND your new credit card balances all at the same time.

Home Equity Loans

Though the interest rates on these credit sources are usually lower, you must understand that these loans are guaranteed by the equity in your home. So if you default on this loan you could lose your house. But if you have a solid and responsible debt reduction plan in place, saving more interest by consolidating balances on a home equity might, and I do mean might, be advantageous.

The entire focus here is on you getting the most from all of your money.

It is all about paying less interest so that you will have more left over in your pocket for further debt reduction or to pay for essential expenses. Interest places a huge load or strain on your finances when a person does not have a lot of money left over at the end of the month.

The horrible thing about credit is often that the people who need it the most are usually the people who can least afford higher interest payments. So if you must use credit, then at least seek out the lowest interest so you place the least amount of strain on your finances moving forward.

Making Yourself Financially Attractive

For starters, let's agree on a few important things. First and foremost, people need to understand what credit is, how to get it and how to use it. Second, credit makes life easier when we use it responsibly. And last but not least, we need a credit card to do some of the things we need to do in life.

The reason we need to agree on all of that is because once we agree that credit is an important part of our lives, we will also understand our need to make ourselves look as financially attractive as possible to bank, credit card companies and other lenders. Because when we are able to accomplish that, life not only becomes easier but it becomes a lot cheaper as well.

Another thing to think about is that we do not live in a vacuum nor are our individual need usually special. The reality is that we are just like most people applying for credit so we are actually competing against them for any available credit.

Because of this, banks, credit card companies and other lenders receive requests every single day for new credit. In many case the requests outpace the need for lenders to lend out their money. It's an example of demand exceeding need or supply at times and when that happens, the lenders are in a position to pick and choose who they lend money to, how much the give them and at what interest rate they pay.

So if we want to get the best chance of approval or get the lowest rate, we have to make ourselves appear to be among the best applicants when it comes to credit. There are several ways to accomplish this and we should keep all of them in our minds as we go through life and use credit.

First and foremost we need to be responsible with credit. That means not using credit for every little purchase and constantly paying interest on money you don't have. While we may need a home mortgage or a car loan, that new purse or fly fishing set-up should wait until we can afford to pay cash.

It also means keeping your payments current and on time for long periods of time. As we have already said, paying everything on time for two or three months is not going to make the lenders come running to you with extra credit. Depending on your situation, you might have to have years of perfect payment history to get your rating back to where it needs to be.

But also keep in mind that years of good history starts with a few good months.

You also want to show some kind of financial and personal stability as well. If you have been married for 20 years and have had the same job for the last 10 years, you would be considered a much better risk than someone who has been married 4 times in the last 15 years and who has had 14 jobs over that same time frame as well. Even though you might have had great reasons for changing jobs so often and even for a few of those divorces, the real problem is that you usually won't even get the opportunity to tell your side of the story. Someone, who doesn't know you at all, will read your application, see your profile and either shred it immediately or forward it on for additional research or approval. You don't usually get to state your case or explain away things.

The best way to approach things like your credit profile is to always look at things from another point of view. IN this particular case, you at your actions and history from the lenders perspective. If you are thinking about changing a job or taking out a loan, ask yourself how this might look to a lender in the future.

If you appear to the lender as someone who is always looking to credit for their day to day needs, that might reflect poorly on you. While it might not preclude you from getting credit, it might result in you being charged a higher interest rate than other people.

Instead, appear to the lender to be someone who uses credit to their advantage and uses it as a tool to get more out of life. In other words, you want to appear to be a person who uses credit and not someone who lets credit use them.

Check Your Personal Information Regularly

We keep track of our weight by stepping on the scale. We don't usually weight until we are morbidly obese to lose a few pounds. We also balance our check book or monitor our bills and expenses every month as well. We don't wait until we start getting overdraft notices. Throughout life we use different ways of getting feedback on how things are going so we can make whatever changes or adjustments that we need to make.

Our credit score should be no different.

Usually you are entitled to see your credit reports once a year at no charge if you ask for them. The three major credit reporting agencies are Experian, Equifax and Trans Union. Each of these might have different information on them because they gather their information in different ways or from different sources. So while seeing one report is good, you really need to see all three in order to get the most accurate picture of your overall credit profile.

There are also websites you can go to where you can purchase your credit reports as well. But before you spend your hard earned money, check with your credit card companies to see what is available to you for free. Free is better and free will not cost you money that you could be using to pay down your debt!

Websites like Credit Karma will give you your credit score for free anytime you want it and this is a great resource to go on a few times a year to make sure nothing major has changed. These days with all the identity theft going on, checking several times a year is something that everyone should be doing.

If you should see entries on your report that you don't recognize, or if you see accounts listed that you don't have, then follow up on these immediately. Sometimes people who steal your information will open accounts in your name and then trash your credit rating. Recovering from this kind of activity can take a long time and be very difficult.

There is one thing to remember when it comes to your credit reports. Getting them is great but if you never look at them or understand what is in them, they won't do you much good. In other words, to get the proper benefits from them you have to read them and use them. It doesn't take long and it can save you a lot of hassle and trouble if you catch things early.

Debt Stays on for 7 years after it is paid

Before we go any further, let's make one thing perfectly clear. You cannot undo a lifetime of irresponsibility overnight. You cannot erase bad behavior immediately by correcting it. We need to not only change our behavior and attitudes but also show that we can continue with that behavior for long period of time.

Don't believe the people who tell you they can get rid of every bad entry immediately because they just cannot do that legally. Granted legitimate mistakes can come off but bad credit stays with your for a while.

There are a lot of people who think they can take the easy way out by declaring bankruptcy. Well, bankruptcy can allow you to start with a sort of clean slate but it is not the easy way out that many people seem to think it is. You cannot declare bankruptcy today and start fresh again tomorrow. It just doesn't work that way.

Debt stays on your credit report even after it has been paid off. Why? Because your credit report is an accounting of what you have done in the past. So, depending on the type of debt you had, it will stay on for a period of years whether it was good or bad for your credit score.

Some types of debt can stay on your credit report for up to 7 years! So even though you might have had some or all of your debts forgiven or reduced, it will still follow you for many years. So any time a lender accesses your credit files they will see that bankruptcy. They will know what you had done before that helped bring you to bankruptcy and they will get an idea of how you really are with credit.

So whenever you are deciding just how to address any kind of debt or financial issue, remember that this decision will follow you for several years. So what you do today can either help or hurt you over the years. Sometimes those so called "debt reduction experts" don't tell you the whole truth and are not really acting in your best interests.

So the best way to deal with credit problems is to deal with them before they make it to your credit report. It is much better to not get the bad debt in the first place than to decide how to address it afterwards. It is better to act responsibly today so you won't have to develop a strategy tomorrow.

Act Sooner Rather than Later

Financial and credit issues are just two of the things in life that really benefit from prompt or pro-active actions. This is because the faster we act, the less damage will happen. The quicker we act, the faster we can get back on the right track. The sooner we correct bad behavior, the more time we will have to correct things.

If you were bringing home $1,000 a month but spending $1,100 a month, your debt would increase by $100 per month plus whatever interest or finance charges you had to pay. So if you discovered this in month 1 you would have to pay back $100 plus charges. But if you discovered this month one but waited until month 6 to make the changes, you would have to pay back $600 plus even more fees, charges or interest! If you waited a year, it would be even more!

Some of us look at negative behaviors and think, actually hope is a more accurate word, that everything will just take care of itself.

Or we think that this was just a fluke or one-time event that will never occur again. Still others will just play ostrich and stick their head in the sand and ignore it.

But when we do nothing, nothing happens. When we change nothing, nothing changes. Whatever we had done, or not done, that helped put us in whatever position we find ourselves in is just going to make things worse. Something needs to happen or get done and it must be done now rather than later in order for it to be the most effective and cause fewer problems.

If we find ourselves now in debt or with a poor credit rating, chances are that it did not happen overnight or because of one foolish or inappropriate action. You are in the position or situation you are in because a pattern of behavior brought you here. So as long as that behavior or attitude remain in place, you will not make any headway in digging yourself out of trouble.

Or, if a miracle does happen and you do find yourself out of debt or trouble you will soon find yourself right back where you started from. So if you want to make a real and lasting change you must make it NOW and you must make it last! This is not up for discussion. If you want something to work, you have to put in the work.

Now some of us might feel that our situation is so bad or so large that we simply cannot do much of anything to make it better.

While in some case that might be true, the vast majority of us CAN make a difference no matter how small, if we just put our mind to it. The absolute worst thing we can do is to do nothing at all.

Using that $100 a month example we used earlier, what might happen if you realized we were overspending but could only reduce our expenses by just $20 a month. Even after that you would still be spending $80 more a month than you brought in. So why bother?

Well, if you do nothing at the end of the year you would be $1,200 plus interest in debt. But if you had saved that $20 at the end of month one you would have saved $220 over the course of the year and you would have ended in debt just $980 plus you would have paid less interest because you had a lower balance! So at the end of the year you would have had approx. $300 less overall debt saving just that $20 a month!

It's like trying to lose weight. You might say you can't lose weight but if you burned 100 calories more or ate 100 calories less each day, which just about everyone could easily do, that would wind add up to 36,500 calories per year which equals roughly 10 pounds! This kinds of puts a different perspective on things just a bit doesn't it?

It's like trying to walk 10 miles. The person who walks just a tenth of a mile a day will complete the 10 miles in 100 days. The person who doesn't walk at all will be in the exact same place 100 days later.

They will be no closer to their goal because they failed to even take the smallest action.

Think about this another way.

If we have any goal, we can either do things that bring us closer to our goal or further away from it. If we take positive steps, the faster or earlier we start the faster we will attain our goal. The more we put things off, the longer it is going to take.

To make matter worse, the things that brought us to this point usually are negative actions like abusing credit or spending too much of failing to live within our budget. So the longer we continue those behaviors or attitudes the further away from our goal we will become. It is like someone who has to get to a place that is 5 miles to the east but meantime he is walking towards the west. Unless he turns around and changes the direction he is walking, the longer he will have to go in order to reach his destination.

Don't put things off. It will just make things more difficult and much harder to achieve. Don't allow destructive or negative behavior continue one minute or day longer than it has to.

No matter how little you can do, do something. No matter how long it takes you to get where you want to be, always make movements in the right direction. It will just make it easier and faster to get where you want to be in life.

How to Fix Errors

on Your Report

OK, let's say you requested a copy of your credit report and you found an error. Something was either wrong, not updated or you have no knowledge of an account in your name at some store or organization. When this happens you need to report it and start the process of having it investigated and hopefully removed from your report.

This will require some investigation and the exchange of certain information between you, the credit reporting agency and the creditor themselves. The easier and faster you can make the process go for everyone the better chance you will have in being ultimately successful.

While we are not credit report specialists or affiliated with any of the reporting agencies here are a few suggestions for you to follow when it comes to getting disputes resolved.

Keep in mind that the resolution you get might not be the one you wanted or expected.

Start a Record

When it comes to resolving any kind of dispute, evidence and paperwork in the rule. Almost nothing will get resolved based on your conversation or comments unless it can be proven or produced in writing.

That means keeping all receipts, paperwork, pay off notices, cancelled checks, e-mails and all other documents. This also helps you get confirmation of doing what was requested of you. Getting things in writing also helps when people refuse to admit things that they said or made commitments about.

The rule here is that if it isn't in writing it probably doesn't matter. If this should ever reach the level of going to court, you will need documentation in writing. Save EVERYTHING related to the inquiry or dispute until after everything has been resolved and the outcome made final in all aspects.

Part of your paperwork should consist of a time line or chronological record of what happened and when it happened. Each entry should have a date and time, the people involved or spoken with and a description of the conversation. If any commitments or noteworthy statements were made they should become part of the record.

Inform the Credit Reporting Agency

Your first step should be to identify the incorrect or questionable entry and contact the agency or agencies that have that entry on their report. If it is on more than one report you MUST contact each agency so that it is removed from all reports. One report may not inform the others so it is better to be safe than sorry.

Be aware that the credit agency is NOT your enemy. They only report what information they receive and they truly want their reports to be accurate. But also be aware that there are people who will do anything and everything to get accurate but damaging information removed as well.

Because of this, have all your information arranged so that it gives an accurate but condensed version of what really happened. In other words, don't take 30 minutes to tell a story that could easily be told in 2 minutes. You want people to help you not get frustrated with you.

They will probably ask for specific information or documentation so write down a list of what they ask for. Then do you best to provide that to them. If you don't have something they need, try to get it. If that is not possible then try to get them whatever you can that pertains to what they asked for and then write a note explaining why what they asked for is not available.

Then find out what the next step is going to be. Ask them what you need to do, if anything, to help the process along. If they are going to take it from there respectfully ask for a time frame as far as how long this should take. Be aware that the process does take time and it often takes more time than one might think.

So be patient and do not hound them for updates until their time frame has passed. Even then, be patient and respectful. Always remember that you need them to make changes that are important to you. The bottom line at this point is that you need their help a lot more than they need to provide it to you. They should not be treated as an adversary at this point.

Inform the Business who Supplied the False Information

If you are asked to do so, contact the credit card company or organization that posted the incorrect entry. In fact, unless you are specifically asked not to contact them, I would contact them as well and make sure you present the case as it should be presented.

Very often you can resolve minor disputes or identity theft issues quickly and easily by presenting certain documentation or signing certain documents. You may also be asked to provide required documentation to prove your position such as pay off notices, receipts and other items. Write down a list and gather the materials.

At this point you should start to get an impression on whether this is going to be easy or if they are going to fight you in removing the inaccurate or negative item. Be advised that if you did miss payments or other things that those entries are not likely to be removed because they are truthful.

If things are going smoothly and they agree that you are correct, ask them to inform the credit agencies and ask for a time frame when this is expected to be completed. Then follow up with them and the credit agencies after that time frame to make sure things have been changed accordingly.

If they are intent on fighting with you it is probably going to take a third party working on your behalf to work with them to get things done. This might be a local consumer agency or a paid representative. You will have to decide which is your best choice based on your own situation.

Make Sure Corrections are Placed in Your Report

If you managed to convince them that the entry was in error, find out how long it is going to take for the changes to become part of your report. Then, after that time frame has elapsed, confirm the deletion or changes with each credit reporting agency. If the changes were made, then you are done. If they have not been made yet, inquire why.

Accept Defeat or Enjoy Victory!

At this point you have either been victorious and have had those incorrect entries removed from your credit report. Hopefully your credit scores will reflect those changes especially if the mistake was pretty serious. If this happens, gather all your paperwork and file it away in case you need to supply it in the future.

If the agency has refused to make the changes because the information has been shown to be accurate, you can either continue to fight it using a lawyer or other professional or you can accept defeat and understand what originally happened that caused this problem in the first place. Then, change what you did throughout the process so it doesn't happen again in the future.

Budgets, Attitudes & Moving Forward

OK, let's all agree that if you had or still have a poor or bad credit rating that it is because of something you did in the past that caused it. Even if you had been the victim of identity theft but it got out of hand because you never checked your credit rating or reports every year, you played a role in the problem. You need to take ownership of this.

Taking responsibility or ownership is important because once we do that, we tend to stop making excuses. When we stop making excuses it becomes much easier to get to the bottom of things and stop the bad behavior that put us where we are or were.

While you cannot change the past, you do have control over the present and what you do now will influence your future.

So now is the time where we stop bad behavior, stop doing the wrong things and start changing damaging behavior and attitudes that helped cause the problems or behavior in the first place.

While we are not financial analysts or financial planners, here are a few things you should think about as we start changing our behaviors and attitudes when it comes to finances and handling credit responsibly:

Know Your Finances

You cannot possibly know what you have to spend every month if you don't know how much comes in and what your standard expenses such as rent, insurance, taxes, cay payments and other expenses add up to. You need to ALWAYS plan on spending less than what comes in so that you will be able to save a little for emergencies and for the future.

It simply does not work to guess as you go through the month. It doesn't take a lot to spend a few hundred dollars more than you should. When you do that it means the next month you will have that much less to spend and that can create a hardship.

Education and information go hand in hand. The more you can base your decisions on fact instead of guesswork, the more accurate and focused your decisions will be. You also need this information to create a budget or debt reduction plan.

Live Within Your Means

This is something a LOT of people either cannot do or refuse to do. We must understand that our income and personal situation will define what type of lifestyle we can live in. If you earn $30,000 a year you cannot expect to live a $100,000 a year lifestyle!

Except that this is exactly what many people do. They feel they are entitled to the same things that their neighbors have even though they earn far less money than they do. So they buy things they cannot afford, create monthly bills far in excess of what they can pay and wind up running up huge credit bills and trashing their credit scores in the process.

People today need a wake-up call. We are not entitled to a certain lifestyle just because we were born into this world. We need to prepare for our future, get the education we need to get the jobs we want, and work hard to be able to afford the lifestyle that we want for ourselves.

That is the correct order when it comes to purchasing things. We need to be able to afford to buy things BEFORE we buy them. We do not purchase things with the idea of one day being able to afford them or just purchase them because a friend or neighbor has them. Live within your means, purchase what you can afford and do not succumb to the entitlement virus.

Learn to Budget

Budgeting is usually one of the most important keys to financial responsibility and debt reduction. We already talked about understanding our finances and how much money we have to work with every month or week. Now we need to take that information and budget it out so we always stay within our means.

Budgeting entails writing down all our fixed expenses and what we currently spend money on to see if we are behaving responsibly. If we are spending less than we are bringing in, then we are in pretty good shape. But if we are spending more than we bring in, changes need to be made and be made quickly.

Budgeting usually contains several envelopes or "buckets" where our money goes every month. You would have a bucket for rent, another for insurance, another for food, and another bucket for clothing. You might have 4 bucket or you might have 24 buckets depending on your own situation. But no matter if you have 4 or 24 buckets ALL those buckets need to add up to less than what you bring in every month.

Then you look at each bucket and you will know how much you have to spend that month. If you have $50 in your entertainment budget for the month and you spend it all the first weekend, go to the library and get some good books because you are not going out for the remainder of the month!

That's how budgeting works! When the money in the bucket is gone, you wait until the bucket gets filled next month.

Budgeting also forces you to look at all the places your money does go and that can be a great thing as well. Sometimes you get your eyes opened when you see how much you spend every month on things like take-out food, dining out, upscale coffee and other things. This can be great because you have highlighted potential areas of savings moving forward so you can have more money left over for other things.

Once you have your budget in place, you really need to adhere to it or follow it. Even the best budget will not do you any good if you don't follow it. So understand your finances, create your budget, fill those buckets and then stick with it!

Get Out of the Spending Mode

This one is more of an attitude adjustment for a lot of people. Most of us are creatures of habit. We do things for a while and they become second nature and we keep doing them even though circumstances around us may change. The result is that even though we are doing the same things that may have worked for us in the past, they are now causing us problems.

For example, if we lived home and were used to spending $400 a week on meals and fun that might have been just fine. But when we bought the house or rented the apartment, our expenses changed.

We might not have that extra $400 anymore. So we need to get out of some of the habits we used to have and change them to reflect our new lifestyle or financial condition.

Another example might be losing your job or having to take a cut in pay. When this happens, the things we used to do might not be possible anymore without going into debt. So we need to get out of the spending mode that caused our problems and transition into other things.

Sometimes we get so in the mode of spending money on things we can easily do ourselves that we can uncover considerable money every month just by changing our spending habits. We could make our morning coffee at home instead of spending $4 for a cup on the way. We could bring our lunch instead of taking out. Those are just a few of the things we might change to make a difference in our spending habits.

Remember, if you want to save more money or pay down your debt there are only two options for you. You either have to spend less or earn more or a combination of both. So decide which option is better for you and then make the changes you need to make to get back on the right track.

Learn to Save

A lot of us feel that the future is too far off to worry about now.

But we are not talking about retirement here. We are talking about preparing ourselves for the little things that life always seems to throw our way.

Things like a furnace breaking down or our car needing expensive repairs or possibly losing our job. These are the things that can throw budgets and our credit into a tailspin. But if we had saved some money to tide us through these unexpected expenses, we can come out of them with our budgets and credit intact.

The rule of thumb is to have 3-6 months' worth of expenses in your savings. Most of us don't have that but we should have something. We should have some money saved so that every little expense doesn't have us reaching for our credit cards and their 18% interest! We should have enough so that we can take life's little adventures and handle them without having to use credit and pay that interest.

Save whatever you can even if it is only a few dollars a month. Every little bit adds up and will help us down the road when problems hit. A lot of people have had times when they wished they had more money. But very few people complained that they had a problem and had too much money.

Keep Track of Your Spending

Sometimes it's a good idea to just keep a record of everything you have purchased over the last month.

Not just major purchases but everything from the rent down to the candy bar you got out of the candy machine at work.

This can be helpful because it really paints a picture of EXACTLY where your money goes. Major expenses we remember but it is the little things that can quickly add up. So at the end of the month when you go over your spending you will now be able to see that you spent $175 on those work candy bars or take out snacks! That might shock you. That is only about $5.50 a day but it adds up fast.

Being able to look at a larger sample of things often gives us a better perspective of what we are spending money on and helps us reduce wasteful spending by making little tiny changes that pay big results. For example, you might spend $1 on that daily candy bar which comes out to $30 a month. But if you bought a box of those bars at the supermarket or warehouse store, you could get them for half the price and save $15 without one bit of sacrifice!

Tracking our spending just gives us another way to understand what we are doing and how it is affecting our finances and credit. This allows us to make better choices and save money without sacrificing the things we like or our overall lifestyle. In other words, it helps us get more out of our money each and every month.

Watch Out for Interest Rates

I'm going to be short and sweet here because it is something we have already talked about.

Moving forward, search out the lowest credit rates and use those sources when you absolutely need to use credit. This will enable you to reduce the cost of interest and give you more money to pay off your balances easier and faster.

Credit

Use credit wisely. Whenever possible pay off your entire balance in full when the bill arrives. No more finance charges or interest payments. This will enable you to stay out of debt longer and help you save more money as well. Remember that every dollar you pay in interest is one dollar that you earned but got nothing for in exchange.

Creating Extra Income

I might be making the wrong assumption here but most of the people who find themselves in credit problems usually got there because they didn't have enough money in the first place. Like we said, you are in credit problems because you either spent too much or didn't make enough. Well, we just discussed how to get more from the income you have by spending carefully and changing some habits so now we are going to tackle the other part of the equation.

Sometimes the only way we can get out of debt is to increase the amount of money coming in every month. We need to do this because no matter how much we might have been able to reduce our expenses, we could not get down to a level low enough that would enable us to become out of debt and self-sustaining.

There are a few different ways for you to bring a little bit more money into your household every month.

Some will require more sacrifice than other but some of them are very easy and perhaps something you should have been doing all along. IN any case, here are a few options you might wish to consider when it comes to increasing your income and improving your cash flow:

Ask for a Raise

If you are a top performer and you haven't received a salary increase in quite a while, perhaps it is time to ask for one. But keep in mind that needing more money is not justification for getting a raise. Get your facts together to show them why you deserve an increase. Make a business case why it is deserved and how much you benefit the company through your work.

The great part about increasing your income in this manner is that you will be bringing more money into the household without working longer. This is something you should do whenever things change and your value in the marketplace changes as well.

Get a Better Job

Sometimes this is easier said than done but sometimes we get too comfortable in a job and we stay in that job far too long.

Moving to a better job may not only give you a larger salary but also provide you with benefits that might reduce your expenses as well. For example, if the new job includes a company car and insurance, you could sell your car and cancel your insurance and save those expenses.

Work Some Overtime

If your job is the type of job where overtime is available, request a few extra hours to bring more money home every month. This extra money can be used to trim down debt or to help you build your savings so that you can handle emergencies.

Get a Second Job

This option takes some time away from your family and might be the least desirable for many people but when you get yourself in financial trouble sometimes you have to do something you don't want to in order to dig yourself out.

Open a Small Business

If you have a marketable skill or talent that enables you to produce products or run a business, why not consider opening a small business. Opening a web-based business is not expensive and you can get up and running in a matter of hours for less than $100.

Though this option is not for everyone, there is a lot of money to be made if you have the right skills and business savvy. If this option interests you, check at the end of this book and join our mailing list where you can find information pertaining to finance and business.

Re-Evaluate your Tax Deductions

Everyone pays taxes and everyone hates to pay taxes. So the next time you do your taxes, make sure you are taking all your deductions that you are qualified to take. Every dollar you save in taxes is one more dollar you will find in your paycheck and wallet at the end of the month.

Part Two:

Steps You Can Take to Raise Your Credit Rating

If your credit rating is kind of low and you want to get it higher, these tips and techniques can help

Steps You Can Take to Improve Your Credit Score

Get a Copy of Your Credit Report

We mentioned this already but make it a priority to get a copy of all three of your credit reports once a year. This enables you to look over your report to make sure there are no false or inaccurate entries on your report. You can also make sure that no one has opened any new accounts in your name that can easily damage your credit score and rating.

Question any Negative or Mysterious Entries

People make mistakes and there might be false or dated entries on your credit report. You might have paid off a loan and that has not been added to your report.

Or you might have been charged for late payments that really were made on time. Don't fall into the trap that makes you think that these are no big deal.

Question and challenge any entry that is not accurate or updated. If there are accounts that you are not aware of, contact those companies immediately and request cancellation. This can be one of the first signs that someone has stolen your identity by accessing private information.

Keep Meticulous Records!

No one is going to listen to you or change anything regarding any financial account unless you have adequate records and documents to support your position. This means you need to get organized and keep receipts and notices regarding any of your loans or credit accounts.

When you make a payment, keep the check or print out a receipt when you pay online. If you pay in person, retain the receipt. Sometimes payments do not get posted or credited to your account for some reason and you will need these documents to prove you made the payment. This also applies to payments made on time that the lender is saying you made late. Having a dated receipt is the only way you will be able to convince anyone that you were right and that you did make the payment on time.

Keep these records for several years even if you have closed the account or paid off the loan. You never know when any piece of information might show up on your report and you might be called upon to produce certain documents long after the loan or balance has been completely paid off.

Amount of Credit Versus How Much You are Using Stay under 30%

Just because lenders give you a credit line does not mean that you should max it out on a regular basis. Lenders look for how much a person has in credit and how much of that available credit they are in fact using. As of this writing the desired percentage of credit actually used as compared to the amount that is available is 30%.

This means that if you have $10,000 in available credit you should only have outstanding balances totally no more than $3,000. Because of this it is usually desirable to have multiple accounts or higher credit limits which might make it easier to stay under the 30% mark.

But also be aware that a more important figure is what you can afford. If you have $100,000 worth of available credit does not mean that it is all right for you to be $30,000 in debt. You still have to pay the interest on that $30,000 so keep that in mind.

Just don't think that you can have one account that is maxed out and still have a good score because you pay the minimum payment every month.

Know Your Credit Scores

You cannot be responsible with credit and not know your credit score. You credit score gives you constant feedback and both how you are doing and the overall "health" of your credit rating. If something should go wrong or someone might have stolen your identity, you might never become aware of this until your rating gets in the toilet.

By that time sufficient damage might have been done so that you cannot get that mortgage to buy your new home or get approved for that auto loan so you could get that new car. Know your score and what goes into it. This should be done on a yearly basis.

It is strongly suggested that you join one of the online sites where you can go to check your credit score often. If you do join one of those sites check your cores every month. They might vary by a few points but if you see a 50 or 100 point drop you should look into why that happened and get it straightened out.

Leave Old Good Debt on Your Report

Some people try to remove old entries on their credit report.

If you have an old loan or credit card account on your report that was paid off in full and on-time, consider leaving that on the report because it is a positive or good entry for you. It shows that you had credit in the past and repaid it responsibly.

Shop for Credit within a Short Time

Sometimes we need to "shop" for credit to get the best rate before taking out a major loan. Prime examples of this might be home mortgages, auto loans, student loans and other larger loans. But you also should be aware that any time someone requests your credit history this can lower your credit rating if there are more than the number of allowable requests.

The idea behind this is that a lot of inquiries might mean that you are planning to open several different accounts and significantly increase your available credit. Since there are various reasons for doing this that are not really positive in nature, the credit card agencies do not like to see many inquiries.

But they do understand that people often do shop for the lowest rates and they sometimes will take this into consideration and will allow multiple inquiries within a short period of time for the same type of credit.

So if you are looking for a mortgage and fill out applications at 7 different bank, this will not be held against you.

To make sure this happens, fill out all your applications within a relatively short period of time so the inquiries will also come in pretty much together. Then the agencies will see these inquiries and recognize them for what they are. People shopping for the best rate and not people looking to access massive amounts of credit for whatever reason.

Pay Your Bills on Time

If this one doesn't make sense then you should close this book and reopen it at page one and start again. If there is one thing you ALWAYS should do with ANY credit account or loan is to make EVERY payment BEFORE the date that it is due.

I recommend making it several days before it is due to give the company a chance to process your payment and apply it to your account before the due date. This can help avoid confusion when you make a payment before the due date but it is posted after the due date. Always give yourself a little "wiggle room" when it comes to payment deadlines.

While the occasional late payment might be overlooked when all other payments were made on time, it is never a good idea to think that a late payment every once in a while is "OK". Always make every payment on time so you never have to wonder if any of those late payments really hurt you or not.

Pay More than the Minimum Payment

The only people who like to see people make the minimum payment are the lenders. That is because the less you pay off each month the more money they make on finance charges or interest. The fact is, that if you pay the minimum payment every month you are pretty much spinning your wheel and are not really getting anywhere in paying off your outstanding balance.

Instead, pay as much as you can every month. Always pay more than the minimum payment whenever you are capable of doing so. But if you are not, make the minimum payment and make it on-time so you will maintain a current and on-time payment schedule.

If You Have Missed Payments, Get Current

If you were behind in your payments in the past and had missed payments, do your best to get current as quickly as possible and then do your very best to create an on-time payment history moving forward.

If there was a unique reason for falling behind you might want to make the lender aware especially if that reason is not long applicable.

Your credit score will go down for missed and late payments. It will also not go back up immediately once you start making on-time payments either.

But as time goes by and you keep making your payments on time you will see your score gradually creep back up to where it should be.

Be Careful Where You Use Your Charge Cards

Sometimes where you use your charge cards is important as well. If you have an excellent rating then you can use your cards wherever and whenever you would like to. But if you have a lower credit score some lenders don't like to see people using them for every day purchases or cards that are used constantly.

But this may change over time as using credit to pay for most things is just so much easier and faster these days most people use them all over. But for those people with credit problems, too much use is not considered a great thing no matter how much easier and faster it might be.

On a much different topic, be careful where you use credit cards as it could have an impact on your safety and security as well. If you are in a bad or suspect area be careful when using your credit cards. Information and card numbers can easily be stolen and then used to purchase other products on your account. Be especially alert whenever you give your card to someone and they go somewhere else to process the transaction. The most common example of this would be waiters and waitresses who take your card from you at the table and then go to the bar for processing the charge.

Check Your Credit Card Statements EVERY Month!

We just mentioned the problem of people stealing your card numbers and then making purchases. This can be done whenever you purchase something over the phone as well. To help identify this type of behavior, check your online credit card statement at least twice a month to uncover charges that you did not make.

Purchases not made by yourself or other authorized users on your account are not your responsibility. But you have to bring them to the attention of your credit card company who will investigate the suspect transactions. The can then be removed from your account if they are shown to be fraudulent.

Request A Fraudulent or Suspect Transaction Be Placed in Dispute

Whenever you dispute a transaction, ask that the amount of the transaction be placed in dispute which means it is not part of your outstanding balance. This allows you to not pay that portion of your bill without a negative entry on your credit report. This can be important because once you give the credit card company your money and have to rely on a refund you lose a lot of leverage with the credit card company.

Set Up Payment Calendars

We all have a lot going on every day and sometimes it is easy to forget which bills are due on which days. The result is that we often forget to pay a bill on time and this can end up costing us late payment charges and even negative entries on our charge cards.

If you have a daily planner or calendar, right each bill's due date on the calendar as a reminder. If you pay bills online, consider setting up auto bill pay for standard transactions that are always the same amount. For other transactions, set up auto alerts on your computer or smart phone to remind you a few days before a bill becomes due.

The great thing is that you usually only have to set these alert up once and then they keep reminding you every month or pay your bills for you every month until you tell them to stop. This allows you to think about other things and not worry about due dates and which bill to pay when.

Keep Balances Low

Lenders do not like to see their customers using up large percentages of their available credit line. This sometimes indicates over extension of credit by the customer. Instead, it is far better to have several lower balances than one huge one. Keep the balances low and generally less than 30% of your overall credit limits and you should be in good shape.

However, if your current financial situation does not allow for any money to be available to pay back your debt then any balance is not necessarily a great idea. Remember that for every dollar you pay in interest or finance charges that is one less dollar you will have to pay off your outstanding balance or to purchase necessities the next month.

Beware of Co-Signing

In the eyes of lenders, co-signing a loan is your guarantee to pay back the money if the main person on the card or the loan does not pay it. Do not take co-signing lightly.

You could wind up in a lot of trouble because of someone else's abuse of credit and that trouble can wind up causing a lower credit score and all the problems that go along with it.

Never co-sign for someone who has shown a lack of stable employment, poor financial judgment and the inability to use credit properly in the first place. Though sometimes very young adults will need a co-signer just because they have not been able to have credit long enough to establish a good credit history, older people who need a co-signer in order to get credit should raise a giant red warning flag.

Though it might be difficult to refuse one of your children or other family member, it is important to understand that co-signing places your own credit worthiness in jeopardy. Credit that you co-sign for will be figured in your overall debt because you are liable for it even though the loan is in someone else's name. So co-signing a loan for Cousin Fred might keep you from getting credit you need for something you want.

Work with Creditors When You Cannot Pay

If you cannot make even the minimum payment because of certain events like losing your job or getting sick and having high medical expenses, do not just ignore your bill and accounts and hope no one notices.

This is the very best way to send your credit rating right smack into the sewer.

Instead, contact them and let them know what is going on. Most creditor will understand this and work with you to void negative entries on your credit report. This is most likely if you have had a really good payment history in the past. If your history was poor to begin with, they might feel that you are making up excuses and that you are not being truthful.

One Bigger Balance is Better than 10 Small Balances

I know that we said that it is not good to run up one account to the maximum and that still applies.

But you also do not want to have 34 cards or loans with balances on them either. Some people do this to make their overall credit look better by not having large balances that might alarm creditors.

But as far as your credit score and rating is concerned a balance is still a balance and having a lot of accounts with balances on them looks bad. Plus, it is a lot more difficult to send off many smaller checks every month to pay those balances off instead of just a couple.

Don't consolidate all your open balances into one large one but it is all right to consolidate several into a couple of accounts to make managing those accounts easier while making yourself look better in your credit profile.

Don't Sign up for a Million Credit Cards

It seems that every day I get a credit card application in my mailbox. Every card has some kind of freebie or special offer to get you to sign up. Maybe it's a free tote bag, a couple of free tickets or the company offers a discount for opening the account in the first place. Whatever the freebie or giveaway is, make sure you really need the account and that it makes sense to open one.

Every account you have is a potential source of credit and the total of that available credit is part of your credit profile.

Having many open accounts with available credit on them might place you at the limit of what lenders want to see you at. When this happens getting a loan or opening an account you really want might be difficult if not impossible.

The lesson here is to open the accounts you need and for all others, make sure the offer for opening an account is really worth it. Personally, a $5 tote bag with the company's logo on it really has limited value to me.

Never "Max Out" any Credit Account

Using up your total available credit on any one account is never a good idea. You should always stay at the 30% level when it comes to using your available credit.

It is OK to go higher in some cases such as when you make a large purchase and intend on paying it, or most of it, off at the end of the month. Creditors understand the need to do this.

But consistently having your credit up to the limit suggests that someone has a difficult time managing their credit and therefore might be considered a higher risk than someone with a low balance. As funny as it might seem, having the same open balance spread across a couple of accounts will look better on your credit report.

But as we said a while back, do not think you can just open more accounts and spread larger balances across more accounts. Creditors will look at all the open accounts and wonder why you need another one. They will see through what you are doing and penalize you for it.

Why Paying in Full Might Be Bad for You!

This one might surprise you a bit. I know it opened my eyes a bit! Paying your statement in full every month might make lenders a little resistant to give you a credit card. Why? Well, one of the ways lenders make their money is by charging people interest or finance charges on their outstanding balances. If you pay off your balance in full every month, you don't have to pay those charges and the company makes no money on interest from you. So in that sense, you might look a bit unattractive.

But consider this before you start thinking you should be paying those poor credit companies some interest every now and then. Credit card companies earn a percentage of every sale you put on your card even when you pay the balance in full every month. Depending on the credit card used those fees can be 3-4% and they are charged to the merchant for the convenience of offering the ability to use a credit card to purchase.

Merchants like it because accepting credit cards increases their sales by a LOT and they just build the fees into their price structure anyway. So even though you are not paying your credit card company any interest, you are paying for those merchant fees in the prices you pay at the register.

Write a "Goodwill" Letter if You Accidentally Miss a Payment

As we often say in life, "stuff happens". Whether it is a loss of a job or other life event or if we just had a brain goof and forgot to make a payment on time, sometimes we might miss a payment or two.

When this happens, and you feel that there was a valid reason for it, write a short note to the company and explain the situation

. Or perhaps you can call the customer service number on your bill and talk to a representative about what happened. Sometimes this will do absolutely nothing but sometimes this can result in them not placing a negative entry on your credit report.

Of course this will only work if you have previously established an excellent payment record in the past. If your payment schedule was previously in the toilet it will likely stay there no matter who you talk to or whatever reasons you provide.

Transfer or Consolidate Credit Card Balances

Sometimes transferring or consolidating balances can be a very effective strategy to reduce credit expenses. If you have high interest accounts with balances open on them, sometimes it can make sense to open a lower interest account, if you qualify for one, and then move your outstanding balances over to that account.

By doing this you can usually save several percent in interest charges. This can really add up over the course of a year or two if that is how long it will take you to pay it off. Remember, for every dollar you don't have to pay in interest that means you have one more dollar to pay off that outstanding balance!

Request a Higher Credit Limit

We have mentioned a few times about how it is not good to max out a line of credit or credit card account. But in some cases, our needs change wand we find ourselves using our credit cards more than we used to. Maybe we bought a house, changed jobs or had some other life change that resulted in us using our charge cards more. We can still pay off the balance but we just use them more for various reasons.

In those situations, sometimes you can call the company and ask that your limit be raised. Credit card companies used to do this automatically once a card holder established themselves as being good credit risks. But if your limit is too low for your usage and you come close to maxing it out or using more than 75% of the limit on a regular basis, getting a higher limit will make you look better on your credit report and sometimes result in a better or higher score.

Create a Debt Reduction Plan

If you have considerable debt, don't think it will pay itself off without having a detailed and specific debt reduction plan. After all, what you are doing brought you into debt and it is foolish to think that continuing the same behavior will now bring you out of it. You need to change something and a plan will help you identify what changes need to be made and how to best go about it.

Your plan should include an analysis of what money is coming in and how much is going out as well as a detailed listing of all accounts, their balances and interest rates. The only way to get out of trouble is to understand how you got there in the first place.

Pay off High Interest Accounts First!

If you have certain accounts that have higher interest rates than other accounts, it makes sense to pay those off first because those are the accounts that charge the most interest or finance charges. You cannot "forget" about the other accounts but if you just pay the minimum on the lower interest rate accounts and pay down those higher accounts faster, you will save money.

Also, if you have a lower interest rate card, place new charge expenses, if you must have them, on the lower interest rate cards. We want to "phase out" those higher interest cards to limit our interest charges during the year. Remember, for every dollar we save on finance charge we have one more dollar to pay down our debt! (Are you getting tired of hearing that?)

Pay off Student Loans

If you have some student loans, you need to pay those off on time as well. Student loans will be reflected on your credit report and how you pay them off will be reflected on your overall credit score as well.

Check the interest rate on those loans to see whether or not you should make them a priority or not. If the interest rate is higher than you other debt, pay these off faster. If it is lower, then pay off higher interest rate debt first while making the minimum payment on your student loans.

Separate Yourself from Bad Credit Co-Signers

It's time to say this again. If people want you to co-sign for a loan than you need to understand that this can be the same as taking out the loan yourself! If the person stops paying the creditors will come after you for payment and you will have no choice but to pay it or have your credit rating slammed as well.

If you have already co-signed a loan, it might be worthwhile to see if you can be removed from that role. If the person has paid off a considerable part of the loan or at least has established a good payment record so far this might be possible. But the best overall strategy is to not co-sign in the first place.

Though it might be difficult, no matter who the person might be if they have bad credit or a reputation for being irresponsible with money and employment, do NOT co-sign a loan for them.

Even if it is a family member and you are being pressured to co-sign, do NOT do it unless you have the funds to pay off that loan as if it was one of your own.

Because it very well could be one day.

Do Not Use One Form of Credit to Make a Payment on Another

I am sure some genius out there figured out that they could use a cash advance from one card to pay the balance of another card and then use a cash advance for the card they just paid off to pay off the first cash advance. Take my advice and do not so this!

When you do stuff like this fees will kill you, balances will go up and you will be digging yourself in a deeper hole every month. Cash advances usually have their own fees associated with them which make the cost of credit go even higher. Which is why we are going to talk about cash advances next!

Stay Away from Cash Advances!

Most credit cards give you the ability for you to use them to withdraw cash from banks, ATM's and other financial institutions.

This is an easy way to get the cash you need when you need it. It is easy because the credit card companies want to make it easier for you because they make a ton of money on cash advances.

First of all, while you may have a grace period on your credit purchases when you pay off your total balance at the end of the month, cash advances offer no such grace period and you start paying those high interest rates from day one. So you are basically paying 18% a year for convenience.

Second, cash advances usually have their own "transaction fee" which really means that for the convenience of them loaning you money for that 18% interest rate, they also feel it is necessary to charge you a few dollars for the convenience. The fee might only be a few dollars but if you do this often those fees can add up!

Cash advances should only be used in emergencies or when you desperately need cash and you have no access to your own funds. That might happen when you are on vacation or out of the area for some reason. But even in those situation if you have some money in the bank even using an ATM and paying the ATM fee will be a more cost effective option than a cash advance.

Stay Away from Your 401K!

One thing we almost never should do is take money out from our 401K or other retirement accounts to pay down our debt. The reason for doing this is two-fold.

First we should not be trying to solve today's problems at the expense of our future. Retirement savings are a critical part of our financial health and you should not touch those for any reason. If you feel you must for some reason, PLEASE consult a financial advisor or your retirement plan manager for guidance before making any transfers.

The second reason is a pretty compelling one. Since you retirement money was probably taken out before taxes all that you take out will become taxable income so you will have to take out much more than what you need to pay off the balance of your credit cards in order to make the payments. For people in the most common tax brackets, that might mean having to take out 30-35% more than you need because of taxes alone! Not only that but the amount you withdraw will count as income and possibly result in you entering a higher tax bracket thus increasing your taxes even more.

Also, if you are not old enough to make withdrawals without a penalty, you will incur another penalty which is probably around 10% of what you withdrew because you took the money before you were eligible to do so for retirement. This couple with the taxes you will have to pay make this a really bad idea most of the time.

Since there are so many factors to consider when it comes to retirement accounts and your current debt, please contact a tax and retirement professional and get some first class advice before you pay those higher taxes and exorbitant penalties.

Personally, I would greatly prefer you take on a second job no matter how distasteful that sounds so that you can earn extra money to pay off your debts instead of ruining your retirement savings.

Beware of Bankruptcy

Please do not think that bankruptcy is the easy way out. Some forms of bankruptcy will stay on your credit report for up to 10 years! Which means that for the next 10 years you will be paying for that bankruptcy in the form of a lower credit score and paying higher interest rates.

Bankruptcy should only be used as a last resort and only after talking with an experienced financial planner or credit counsellor and exhausting other options. No matter what they might say on those commercials on television, bankruptcy is not as simple or as easy as they make it out to be. I'm not saying it isn't the best option for you. I am just saying you need to talk to qualified people before making such an important decision.

Part Three:

Re-Establishing Good Credit

How to get back in good credit
standing after your credit was
in the dumps!

If Your Credit History is Bad, Start to Re-Establish Yourself

OK, for whatever reason your credit was in the dumps but you realize it and want to do something about it. Well, first of all, let me congratulate you for getting this far. You have reached an important step in the credit process and the good news is that all is not lost and that you can regain a good credit rating after a while if you do certain things correctly.

There are a couple of things to remember as we get started to make sure we have the best chances of success and that this success lasts for decades not just a year or so. We want to create lasting change so we don't find ourselves in the same position, or possibly worse, a year or two from now.

First and foremost, we need to understand that we can no longer do the same things that brought us to this point. If our credit is bad or poor it is that way for a reason. Those reasons can no longer exist if we want to re-establish ourselves with a good credit rating. If we want better results, we need to take better actions.

Second, be prepared to go through a little bit of harder times as we get started. This is because, as a person with poor credit, you are likely only going to qualify for higher interest credit accounts. You may have no other choice. But the fact is that in order to re-establish a good credit rating and score, you have to show that you can use credit responsibly. So if a high interest account is your only option, you need to take it.

But higher interest rates mean that you will be paying higher costs for interest if you carry a balance from month to month. So you really need to make a serious effort to NOT carry a balance. You will need to pay off your ENTIRE balance every month. This will save you those high interest charges and we all know what that means!

Paying off your balance every month means that you will probably have to charge less and spend less. This might be difficult but sometimes it is easier than you might think. But whether it is easy or difficult, it has to be done. As we said, you cannot continue to spend like you did when you got yourself in debt.

Attitudes about finances and money may need to be changed as well. This is the time to be totally honest with yourself and admit to your mistakes and actions that caused your credit problems in the first place. This means taking responsibility and acknowledging the things that you did that put you where you are.

This is important because there are things about yourself that are going to have to change and admitting those things exist is a very important first step. Once you know why something went wrong you can take the steps necessary to make sure it doesn't happen in the first place.

I urge you to plan for long-term results but think short-term, at least in the beginning. By that I mean creating a plan and changing your behaviors so that they benefit you for the loan haul but focus on what you are doing on a month to month basis.

Focus your thoughts and efforts on just getting through the month without adding to your outstanding balances and instead reducing them. Don't think about where you will be next year because that could get to be overwhelming especially in the beginning. Focus on what you can do this month, even just for today, to make things go easier on you I the future.

That means evaluating every purchase and asking yourself "Do I really need this?" or asking yourself is there any other way I can get what I need in a more responsible manner? That might means getting a regular cup of coffee at the corner convenience store instead of that Venti Schmenti double foam, ultra latte, super grande double expresso at $5 a pop.

Our progress, or lack of, is not usually the result of one huge action. Instead it is the overall result of many little tiny things that we do over time that provide the bulk of our success. Saving a dollar or two a few times a day can really add up at the end of the month. This is where the real progress is made.

As we start to rebuild our credit, we should have two objectives. The first is to get started on the right path to financial stability. That is our short-term goal. In order to achieve this we have to change behaviors and that usually requires some kind of constant motivation. The best form of motivation is to see positive results from our efforts. That is why we first look for short term success.

If you manage to get through the first week or the first month and realize that you paid off your outstanding balance, saved some money and perhaps paid of some of your debt, you will see the benefits of doing what you were doing. In your mind this will validate all that you did. Now you can set your sights on doing the same things for the next month. When you get through that month, you start focusing on the next one and so on and so on.

As we go on from month to month, those changes that we made start to become habits. In other words we just do them without thinking about them or feeling any hardship or stress about them. They now occur almost by themselves without any thought from us. When this happens we have reached an important step in rebuilding our credit.

Every month that we pay our bills on time and reduce our outstanding credit will help our scores go higher and our credit reports get less negative and more positive. Every payment that arrives on time and not late will be a positive mark for us. For every month we show this type of behavior we will have increased our pattern of good credit management.

More important, for every month we do what we are supposed to do the more normal all of this becomes for us. This means we are less likely to fall back into new habits because we have replaced those bad habits with financially sound habits. Our poor habits before are gone and replaced with good habits.

This is all part of a process. A process that takes place over months and years. It is started by the realization that change must occur because something is wrong. It is started by realizing what we had done wrong in the past and changing those behaviors.

The process then takes on a life of its own as we go from month to month improving our credit, reducing our debt and getting ourselves back to where we need to be in our financial lives.

In the next few pages we are going to give you a few ideas of how you can go from bad credit to good credit in a financially secure and 100% legal fashion. There are good options out there for most of us but they do take time. If someone says they can rehabilitate your credit instantly PLEASE head for the door! Now is not the time to put all your hopes and dreams into the hands of a con artist that will do nothing more than take your money and possibly get you into more trouble.

Consider Using Secured Credit Cards Instead

If your credit was, or currently is, really bad, you might not qualify for a credit card at all. This can be a problem because the only way you can improve or rehabilitate a credit score is by showing that you are capable of using credit responsibly. The only way you can show them is by having an open credit account you can use and pay off.

A Secured Credit card might be an option that is available to you. These are easier to get because they aren't really "credit" cards at all. A secured card is a card that you pre-fund with money from your bank account. Then as you use the card the money is withdrawn from your account.

For example, you open the account and you send them $500 from your bank account. You now have a "credit limit" of $500 which you can use like you would a normal credit card.

As you charge things to the card that balance goes down. When it gets near $0 then you will have to send them more money to replenish your account so that you can continue to use the card.

Secured cards offer certain advantages to the person who need to rehabilitate their credit.

First, since they require you to fund the account, they are of limited risk to the credit card company. Because of this it is much easier to get approved for these kinds of cards. This will enable you to have the card, enjoy the ability to pay with the card and help you re-establish your credit rating.

Second, since you are in fat paying for things in advance when you fund the account, there is no worry about charging more than you can afford or being surprised at the end of the month. Just the fact that you need to keep track of your charges so you know when to replenish will give you a certain amount of awareness when it comes to how much you spend.

Third, though there may be fees associated with s secured card, you will still not have to worry about paying those extremely high interest rates associated with credit card for high risk people. This can save you a ton of money over the years.

There are also downsides to these cards as well though most of them concern the overall convenience of using credit cards.

First, you are limited to the amount that you funded the account with. So they are not likely to be a good option for those who making large purchases.

Second, they are not great for emergency purchases that exceed the amount you funded the card with. You cannot use them when you need something but don't have the money to pay for it. So your flexibility will be limited. But if you have a hard time limiting your credit card purchases, this kind of forced limiting may be a good thing.

After you have shown the ability to use credit responsibly you may be able to transition to one of the higher interest actual credit cards with a credit limit. But be very careful not to get overextended on those cards. Higher interest rates will kill you on interest charges and make saving money or paying down your debt that much more difficult.

Secured cards are an interesting way to show the ability to use credit properly and responsibly. While they do have certain limitations, they also can help you develop good habits through those same limitations. You can check online or go to a local bank to find out where you can go to get a secured card in your area.

Create a Budget

Please don't groan "Oh, here they come again with the budget thing" because having a budget is the single most efficient and best way to get your finances straight and keep them that way. Budgets help because they require specific information that you need to have and become aware of. Without being aware of certain information you will never be able to sustain good credit management.

In their most basic form, budgets are ways to track what comes in and how it goes out when it comes to finances. In order to create a balanced budget, the income that comes in must be the same or more than the expenses going out. There is no way it can work if it is the other way around.

But when you are rehabilitating your credit your budget has a few challenges that might not exist in other people's budgets. That is because if your credit is poor or bad you likely have some debt to pay off and you are likely paying some pretty decent finance or interest charges as well.

If that sounds like your situation then you not only have to budget for your normal day to day expenses you also have to factor in your ability to pay down your debt, pay the finance charges and also setting a few dollars away in savings for the future and to take care of emergency or unexpected expenses. All of these things likely will require special consideration when it comes to your budget.

The first part of any budget is to determine how much is coming in every month. So take a sheet and write down your take home pay plus any other form of income that you might have. Add all of those together to arrive at your total monthly take home income. This is the money you have to work with every month. This is the number that you must not exceed each month.

Now write down all of your fixed monthly expenses as they stand right now. Fixed expenses are expenses such as rent, mortgage, taxes, insurance, utilities, phone, cable, and anything else that has an established monthly payment. Include your minimum payments on your outstanding credit balances. Subtract these expenses and find the figure that represents what is left for everything else you spend money on.

Now figure out what you spend on your food, gas and other expenses. Be honest and accurate. Don't write down less than you really spend.

This is your budget and it should be as accurate as possible. If you buy it, write it down. Subtract this from your income that is left over from the previous expenses.

The last part of your expenses would be expenses that you would have throughout the year but not necessarily every month. These might include medical expenses, prescription drugs, clothing, auto repairs and similar expenses. Figure out what those costs are for the year and divide by 12 to get a monthly figure. Subtract that from your available funds. This is the amount of excess cash you will have to pay down your debt and finance charges as well as saving for the future to build up your cash reserves so you do not have to rely on credit during emergencies.

Hopefully you are positive in terms of cash flow at this point. If you are in the negative, you are going to have to go back and decide which expenses you can cut out or reduce I order to get you back into a positive cash flow. More on that in a bit.

If you have any money left over, try and pay down your debt while building a bit of savings at the same time. While I do understand that you are paying high interest on your balances, it still makes sense to save a few dollars every month to get some kind of financial reserve or cushion for future purchases or situations.

If you have a considerable amount of income left over that's great!

Pay down your debt faster and start being more financially responsible moving forward. But if you are just about even, or just slightly ahead, that might be a little bit too close for comfort.

Every reasonable budget has some kind of provision for unexpected expenses. We need this because those expenses are a part of life for everyone. The worst part is that you cannot plan for those expenses because you often have no idea when something is going to break or when you might need some medical attention. So we have to build those costs into our budget.

In other words, if you bring home $2,000 a month and your budgeted expenses total $1,997, that is not a reasonable or sustainable budget. Any additional expense will throw your budget out the window. So if that is what your budget looks like, it is time to reduce certain expenses.

Nothing is Non-Negotiable!

When you look at reducing expenses, a common mistake is to think that certain expenses are must haves and cannot be touched. That is just not the case. EVERYTHING must be placed on the table for evaluation. NOTHING should be held back. If you have to pay it, you should take a long and hard look at it.

You might not need that 4,000 channel cable package. You don't really NEED a cell phone unless you need it for work. You certainly don't need a home phone and a cell phone, right? You need to eat but you don't NEED to eat out. You can buy food at the supermarket and cook at home at a fraction of the price.

Even when it comes to certain fixed expenses nothing should be held back. You have to pay rent (unless you can live at home) but you don't necessarily have to live where you live now. Maybe you need to move to a smaller house or a less expensive one somewhere else where rents and houses are cheaper.

You might be able to save on utilities by turning the thermostat down or up a bit to save on heat or air-conditioning. Sometimes a simple and small change can save you a bunch of money every year. Since every dollar counts, nothing should be kept off the table.

When it comes to clothes you need pants and a shirt but you don't NEED designer clothes that cost 12 times more and usually don't last as long either. You can get a quality pair of shoes for $75 instead of those designer shoes that set you back $250. As for that purse you paid $500 for because it had someone's name on it, you could get a really nice one that will last for less than half the price.

As I said, we have choices to make and we can make the right chances or we can make the wrong choices. The choice is ours and ours alone.

Budgets Are Works in Progress!

Once you create a budget, you are not done. Things change in life and budgets need to be updated and adjusted to accommodate those changes. Prices go up, needs change and the amount of money we need to get through the month changes as well. Hopefully our income will change as well to keep pace with those expenses.

That is another reason we should have a bit of a cushion in our budgets as well. If something goes up in price, we need to be able to absorb that price in our budget or know how to use or require less of that item so the overall cost stays the same. Sometimes we will have a choice as to what to do while other times change will be dictated to us. Either way, we need to adapt.

So take out your budget every quarter and see if it is still reasonable and accurate. If it is, that's great and we can continue to do the things we have been doing. But if something has changed, change the budget accordingly while still keeping it balanced. If one thing increases, then we need to decrease something else so our overall expenses remain the same. This is what is commonly referred to as balancing a budget.

Budgets Need to Be Achievable!

Budgets need to be accurate but they also have to be achievable.

Just because you place something down on paper does not mean it is realistic and achievable. I can budget $15 a month for food but there is no way I could eat for an entire month for just $15! In reality, I might have to spend 20 times that in a normal month. So just writing down a figure does not make it real.

We all need to take sacrifice into consideration as well. If a budget requires too much sacrifice then we are far more likely to abandon it than if it was more reasonable. So we need to design a budget that is based in reality and that is achievable. It should be something that allows us to achieve our goals while not causing us unusual amounts of pain and hardship. It should be something we can stick with for the long haul so we can achieve our long-term goals.

So when you create your budget, make it accurate, make it honest and make it achievable. Doing so will give you a far better chance for long term success than an overly restrictive will ever provide. Remember, we are in this for the long haul with long term success as our end goal.

Last, but certainly not least, is that budgets only work when you pay attention to them and follow them to the letter. Even the best and most accurate budget will be useless if you just put it in a drawer and forget about it. So since you took the time to create it, now go ahead and use it.

Seek the Advice
of a Financial Planner
or Credit Counsellor

Sometimes no matter how smart we try to be, we just do not know enough about certain things so that we can make the right decision. Sometimes we make what we really think is the right decision only to find out later on that we forgot or wasn't aware of something else that would have caused us to do something else entirely.

They say the road to ruin is paved with good intentions and sometimes that is the case. It is not enough to want to do the right thing. What matters is that we wind up really doing the right thing and not making the wrong decision. This is important because with financial matter the wrong decisions could cost us a lot of dollars in fees and lost income.

Individual finances might seem like a pretty basic process but in reality it can be quite complex. Once you figure in taxes and penalties and this kind of account versus that kind of account and who should shelter their money where it can all get pretty overwhelming. There is simply too much to know and too many details to remember.

This is precisely why we have credit counsellors and lawyers and accountant who specialize in credit problems and individual finances. These people can help you decide which is the best course of action for your specific situation. People are different and their situations are all different as well. Contrary to what you may hear, there is no cookie cutter approach to finance management.

While I realize that there is an expense in hiring or consulting with these professionals, sometimes that expense is well worth it. If you hire a good individual, you will have a financially responsible plan that you can act on. A plan that will take taxes, interest and finances as well as your debt all into consideration. This can help you get better results in less time which will could save you a lot of money.

Think about the costs of hiring someone knowledgeable in all these areas against the possibility of making the wrong choice or making a decision that could cause you to pay more fees, penalties or taxes. Sometimes the taxes alone might be more than a consultation with a professional.

Now this does not mean that everyone should contact and retain a financial advisor. While the decision ultimately is yours, generally speaking the worse your situation is, or the more complicated, the more reason to consult a professional. If you even remotely thinking or contemplating bankruptcy, PLEASE talk to a financial advisor first before making such a major decision!

Depending on where you live and the services available to you, there might be government or local credit counselling services or programs available to you. These can also be run by local charities or public service groups. These programs can run anywhere from debt counselling to financial fitness classes that will teach you how to manage money so that you can get the most out of what money you have.

Some of these programs have credit counsellors that can work with you to help you manage your debt and make suggestions on the best ways for you to resolve your problems. This can be very helpful because having a fresh set of eyes that are not involved in the problem can shed new insight into what is really going on. Plus, they usually will have a more in-depth knowledge of tax codes and credit rules and regulations as well.

I would suggest everyone with credit problems either past or present look into some of these courses. Most of them are free or very low cost and they just might hold the answers to some of your problems. After all, you are just investing your time and you could possibly learn a lot from one or two of these programs.

Another source of possible course could be your local adult education or public library. They often hold courses or seminars on various topics from credit management, debt reduction and retirement planning.

At least check them out to see if there are any of these courses in your area.

Create an Emergency or Liquid Reserve Fund

We touched on this before and we cannot stress the importance of creating a safety net of funds to help you through unexpected expenses moving forward. These are funds you dedicate and save for to help you avoid having to resort to using credit to pay for things you didn't plan for.

Liquid funds are funds that you can access very quickly like from savings accounts or checking accounts. Generally these are funds that if you needed them today or tomorrow you could easily access them. We are talking cash her usually not stocks and bonds.

However, today with all the on-line banking and financial services, you might have more options than ever before when it comes to creating liquid funds. Check with your bank or your broker to see what might be the best fit for you.

Ideally they say that the average person should have 4 to 6 months' worth of income to hold us through almost all emergency needs with the exception of health issues. The idea is that if we lose our job we will probably find another one within six months. If we have to replace a car or an appliance we will be able to access funds to start the process of replacing most of those kinds of things.

Now we understand that 6 months' worth of income is not a trivial amount and might be above the resources of most people. We get that. But just because you cannot get 6 months of income set aside does not mean you shouldn't try for 2-3 months or even one month's worth of income.

Anything that you have available to you when you need it will help you get through a set back or unforeseen expenses. Whether it be $10,000 dollars or $500 dollars, whatever you have saved will mean that much less you will have to put on your credit.

Try and put a little bit aside every pay period and gradually build up your reserve fund. The only exception to this might be if you have a revolving line of credit such as a home equity line of credit that you can access during an emergency. If you have access to that kind of credit you might want to concentrate on paying down your debt to reduce your finance charges and fees.

If you have any concerns about whether or not you are prepared for your future, please consult a financial planner or other qualified individual to help you make the right decision for your particular situation.

Part Four:

Making Credit Work for You!

Making Credit Work for You!

Up until now we have been talking about the fees YOU will pay and the services YOU will receive but now let's turn the tables around a bit on the credit card companies. Now we will look at how you can use your credit cards to give YOU some free bonuses!

All of these bonuses only make sense if you continue to use your credit responsibly and pay off your balance at the end of every month. If you cannot do that at this time then any bonus you are likely to get will wind up costing you more than it is worth.

But if you have to use credit and there is no way around it, as long as the fees are not too high, getting a credit card with some kind of bonus or reward program might help you save some money in the long run. Just keep your eyes open and think things through before making any commitment.

Remember any bonus is only good if you have a need for the bonus and will actually use it. Otherwise you might find yourself paying a premium price to receive something you will never use or take advantage of. If you are not certain that you will use a particular bonus or reward, opt for cash back bonuses instead. Everyone can use cash.

Here are a few things you can do to help credit help you:

Credit Card Yearly Fees

While most credit cards today do have yearly fees, you often will have some control over the fees you pay and the benefits that you will receive. Sometimes there is a trade-off between paying higher fees and receiving more benefits and paying lower fees with getting fewer benefits.

Basically what you want to do is get the best deal for you and your own situation. If you have outstanding debt and poor credit you might have limited options but you probably would want the lowest fees and interest rates to help you pay down your debt as quickly as possible.

But if your credit score is high and you have the need for other benefits and perks then a higher fee with more benefits might be right for you. There is not cookie cutter or one size fits all answer when it comes to what fees or cards are the best ones for you. That decision is usually up to you.

Of course, if you feel that bonus points or other rewards are not things you would be interested in, there might be cards available without a yearly fee. Those might be the best for your own personal situation. There is no one perfect answer for everyone when it comes to cards, fees and benefits. But just make sure when it comes to free cards that they are not charging you higher interest in place of the yearly fee. That interest could wind up costing more than the fee if you do have to pay interest or finance charges.

Credit Card Bonus Points & Perks

Many cards today offer rewards points or cash back bonuses. Both of these are determined by how much you have charged on your credit card. These bonuses might have real value for you depending on your needs.

The rule of thumb here is that if a particular card offers something you need or want, then it might be worth considering. But getting a bonus for the sake of getting a bonus is not a reason to use a particular card or pay a particular fee. If you aren't going to use the bonus it is foolish to pay for it.

For example, my wife and I chose to pay a premium fee to upgrade one of our charge cards to get more airline miles. We have gone to Hawaii 7 times over the last 20 years and have never paid for a ticket. We used our points instead.

So those points had a real value for us. We figured the fee of $100 per year saved us roughly $500 per year when you factored in the free airline tickets.

For those of you that don't travel or don't fly, there are cards with cashback bonus problems where you get a cash rebate based on your purchases. The more you charge the larger your rebate. So this program might be worth a higher fee for you as well.

But regardless of whether you get points or miles or cash back, you should not overuse your card or rack up huge bills you cannot pay just to get a reward you cannot afford to use. After all, if you get 2% cash back but are paying 18% interest on your outstanding balance, that 2% is a really bad bonus!

Bonuses are good for you if you pay off your balance every month. If you do that and all you are paying is the yearly fee, then bonus programs can work very well for you. But if they cause you to charge too much and pay more interest, that's the type of bonus no one really needs.

The Grace Period

If you can really manage your credit EVERY month and pay your balance off in full then something called a grace period might be something that can really help you out.

A grace period is the time between when you charge a purchase and when you actually have to pay for it.

The time between those two dates you actually have the loan of that money for free. Keep in mind that when you carry an outstanding balance every month, or when you make a cash withdrawal there is no grace period and you pay interest or finance charges for every minute you have their money or credit.

But if you pay off your bill in full every month, you sometimes can get "free" money for up to about 6 or 7 weeks if you time purchases right. Here's how this usually works:

Let's say your billing period starts on the first day of the month. So on June 1, you purchase a sound system on your card for $2,500. You will not receive the credit card bill for that purchase until July4 or 5 depending on how long the credit card company take to get it to you. By this time you already have had the use of that money for a month. But you still have about 3 weeks to pay that bill by the due date. If you pay the bill in full by the due date, you do not pay any interest or other charges on the use of that money! So it is like getting a 7 week loan for free!

This can help you make purchases when you need them instead of when you have the money for them as long as you definitely will have the money in a few weeks.

For example, if you need to go food shopping now because your pantry is empty, even if you don't have the $100 for food you would have when the bill comes due. So there is no need to go hungry until your next paycheck comes.

Or if your car needs tires you can charge them and then get the money together over the next few weeks to pay for them. You don't need to take out a loan or ride on unsafe tires until you save up the money.

But if you decide to use this feature you MUST be very careful and not over extend yourself or charge more than you are able to pay back by the time the bill is due. If you cannot pay in full then you will have to pay finance charges and here is something most people are not aware of is that when you do not pay in full the finance charges start FROM THE DATE OF PURCHASE and NOT from the point you started carrying over a balance!

So remember that sound system you purchased on June 1st? If you paid it off in full on July 20th, before the due date, you would have paid no interest or finance charges. But if you only paid off half of that amount? You would now be charged interest on the ENTIRE amount from the date of purchase or June 1ST.

To make matters worse, any other purchases you might have made over that time would also incur full interest charges from the date of the purchase. You cannot separate purchases and pay only finance charges or interest on some purchases. It is all or nothing!

For example, if you bought that sound system for $2,500 and you made 25 other purchases for an additional $1,000, you would have to pay off the entire $3,500 bill before it is due to avoid any interest charges.

So you should be able to easily see the importance of paying your entire balance before the due date to take advantage of the grace period and the interest free loan feature. If you can effectively manage your credit this can help you make purchases more on your schedule than on your paychecks schedule. But if you cannot pay on time, then the grace period for you will no longer exist.

Also be aware that there is no grace period when it comes to cash advances. On cash advances you pay full interest charges from the date of withdrawal to the time a payment is received by the credit card company. Sometimes paying those off in full can be difficult because interest is added every day so you will actually have to pay more than what is shown on your bill because interest would have been added since the bill was prepared and mailed out. The best way to handle this is to make the payment in person at the bank if it is convenient. Or you could call the company and ask what the pay-off amount would be if you paid it off on a certain date. Then you would send a check or make an electronic payment for that amount. If you did overpay a bit it would just be a credit on your next statement.

Added Warranty Protection

This feature is not available on all cards or from all types of cards but it is getting more popular and it can save you a bit of money as long as you can pay off your balance in full by the due date. In fact, this is one feature that actually makes it better for you to charge something even though you might have the cash on hand.

Some credit cards will give you additional warranty periods on your purchases when they are made with your credit card. For example, if you bought a large screen television on your credit card and the television had a one year warranty, the credit card would give you an extra year free. Since most defects show up within the first year or two, you might be able to skip the extended warranty and save yourself a couple of hundred bucks.

Of course, these savings will only happen to the full extent when they are not accompanied by finance charges. For example an extended warranty might cost you $200 but if you charged a $3,000 television and couldn't pay it off, at 18% (1.5% per month) you would pay almost $80 after 7 weeks if you didn't pay it off in full. If you took several months to pay off the television your savings would be much less. If you added more purchases to your card you would also be paying interest of those purchases as well so the actual savings would be even less.

But even though you might be paying finances charges, the value of the extended warranty might still make the entire purchase attractive enough to charge to your credit card. You could tell yourself that while you were paying interest or finance charges you were getting something equal to or more valuable in exchange. Just think about it carefully to decide which is the best option for you.

Anti-Fraud Protection

Let's face it, no matter how safe your credit card company tells you that your information is, it can be stolen. Your credit card has numbers on it that can be read and written down by unscrupulous clerks and wait staff. Unless your card also has a PIN (personal identification number) all they need are the numbers on the card to make purchase on your account.

Because of this, people are a little afraid of the potential effects on the credit rating and their outstanding balance. They are afraid of opening up a credit card statement and seeing thousands of dollars for purchases they didn't make. The sad thing is that these people are not paranoid because this stuff has happened to people many times.

So providing fraud protection to card holders really benefits both the credit card company and the card holder.

The card holder gets protection from unauthorized use of their cards and the credit card companies get their customers feeling comfortable and secure enough that they will continue using their credit cards to make all kinds of purchases. So it is a win-win for all concerned.

I like the anti-fraud protection that credit cards offer mainly because it is getting so difficult these days to spot legitimate companies and websites from the scammer sites. They look exactly the same and sometimes you can stare at them for hours and not see a single thing wrong. But you click on one, your data is captured and your own version of financial hell breaks loose!

The important thing to understand is that customers are not held liable for fraudulent purchases made on their account. These charges, once they are determined to be fraudulent are removed from your account and the credit card company either reports them to the authorities, back charges the merchants involved or just writes them off as a cost of doing business. Whatever they do is not concern of your. All you are interested in is that you do not have to pay for them!

Some people seem to think that doing business over the internet is the only way your data can be stolen. That is just not true. While the internet is often considered to be a scammer or crooks playground, the simple fact is that your data can be stolen in-person off your card, over the internet through scamming sites and sometimes by direct hacking of a company's computers!

So even if you keep your card in your wallet, never us it online and only buy products at businesses that employ only close friends and family members, you data is still vulnerable! That is why fraud protection is so important when it comes to using credit cards.

I would like to say that all credit cards come with this protection and most of them do have it in one form or another. But ALWAYS check whenever you get the terms and conditions of your particular cards, and when you apply for new ones, to make sure this protection still exists. You do NOT want to use a credit card, or even leave the account open and valid, if there is no fraud protection.

We should also state that fraud protection only exists when you follow their policies and procedures. This means notifying them of suspicious or false purchases and also making them aware of lost or missing cards as soon as you notice them. You cannot report the card missing after 6 months and tell them you have 6 months of fraudulent purchases! You need to follow their procedures and policies in order to be protected.

This is because there will always be a group of people who will try to worm their way of paying for things they really did purchase. If you are thinking about that just stop right there.

The credit card companies to not just take your word for it. They research each reported transaction and look for clues as to whether this is a legitimate claim or not.

They might look to see where the transaction took place. For example, if there are purchases made in California and New York within a few hours of each other it would appear that this was highly unlikely or impossible that someone could be in both those places at the same time. Or if the purchase was made in another country while you were in your country that would help as well.

How they research and determine whether or not something is fraudulent is really none of our concern as long as we remain honest and truthful with the credit card companies. After all, this protection is there for our use and we do not pay anything extra for it. It is included in our yearly fees. But once we are found to be dishonest and report real charges as fraudulent, you run the risk of having your account closed, you could be subject to legal problems and you might ruin your chances of ever getting credit in the future. Or at least for 10 years while it stays on your report.

Dispute Resolution Assistance

While this is not technically a feature of having a credit card, it is still a benefit even though it is not listed in writing. One thing that can be very difficult today is getting a store or a manufacturer to stand by their products and service.

It sometimes feels like we are fighting a losing battle when it comes to resolving a dispute.

This is usually because the company already has our money and they might feel that they have little to gain by giving it back. They might not really care that you are dissatisfied or unhappy with them because they already have a lot of customers and losing one really won't make much of a difference.

But for us, we have spent our hard earned money and either received a defective or inferior product or maybe we never received the product at all. Maybe we paid for a service and we got a really poor job instead of the quality service we expected and paid for. In either case we are unhappy and appear to have little recourse.

But if we had charged that product or service, we can ask the credit card company to withhold payment and refund our money. The credit card company will then intercede on our behalf and request the company give a refund. Now even though the company might have refused our request, the game now has changed because we now have more leverage.

The credit card company wants our business. They want us to be happy using their cards and their service.

So they are going to request the refund on our behalf and they are going to expect it be issued as long as our complaint has merit. The company might still not want to give the refund but now instead of offending and angering just one customer they are making an important member of their business unhappy.

We represent just one customer that the company might easily afford to lose. But if they lose the ability to accept credit cards because the credit card company does not like the way they do business, that can REALLY hurt the company. They won't be losing just one customer, they might be losing tens of thousands of customers!

This is called leverage and when we purchase with our credit cards, we have far more leverage than whenever we pay cash or by check. So this is a benefit that can help us get the resolutions we expect and are entitled to.

Another benefit is that when we do have a problem that we cannot resolve on our own, we can also set aside the amount we paid for the product or service until the issue has been resolved. This is another part of the leverage we have over the company. A very important part of leverage.

A credit card company cannot only request the refund, they can withhold payment even when the company refuses their request. The credit card company can issue the refund and take the proceeds out of the company's account. At this point the dispute is between the credit card company and the manufacturer or business that is involved.

Do you think they are going to battle with the credit card company? Of course they're not! They are not about to risk angering and losing a company that probably processes over 75% of their business transactions. So the partner we have in our fight is not only stronger and larger, it probably wields a tremendous influence over most of the businesses we deal with.

It is a nice friend to have on our corner.

Part 5

Building a Secure
Financial Future!

Building a Secure Financial Future!

At this point, you are probably the most aware of credit and the credit process as you are ever likely to be. You now have access to a lot of information that is deigned not only to help you get out of trouble but also will help you rehabilitate your credit rating and get you back to where you need to be.

Hopefully you took advantage of some of this information and have already made a few changes or taken a few steps to turn things around. If you haven't done that yet, it is not too late. Put this book down and get started doing what you need to do. But if you have already started, I would like to congratulate you. You have already done important things that many, possibly most people, would never do because they were either too difficult or would require an admission that they had messed up somehow in the past.

But not you because you have taken action. Heck, just reading this book showed a willingness to learn and required an admission that something wasn't as it should be. So with all this in mind, now we turn the corner and start looking at the future. Because while we can't change the past, we can change what we do now and moving forward. So our future hasn't been written yet.

So let's see what we can do now to help write the future we want to create right now. Here are a few things you need to be aware of to help you create the financial future you want and to help you avoid common problems and mistakes.

Beware of Identity Theft

There are people in this world who exist just to try and separate you from your hard earned money. These are people who steal your money, your financial data and eventually your identity.

Today with so much of our financial lives done online or protected by passwords, it has become far easier to steal from people than it used to be. Lack of physical contact and in-person transactions make it easy for anyone who knows you log-in or personal information and your passwords to take what you have worked long and hard for.

Fortunately, there are a few things you can do to help make this process even more difficult than it really is. Here are just a few of the ways you can protect yourself against identity theft:

Chose Difficult Passwords

Do not use simple or very easy to figure out passwords. It is amazing that one of the most common passwords is the word "password"! Stay away from your name, birthdate, anniversary or your children's names. Mix in capital letters and a couple of symbols or special characters as well to make your passwords extremely difficult to figure out.

Have Multiple Passwords

Most of us have multiple online log in's and mostly we use the same password. While that is understandable because it is easy to remember, just realize that if a hacker figures out your password at one site or account they will try that everywhere else as well. To avoid this, create multiple passwords.

You can use shorter or easier to remember passwords for less critical account or applications that can do you little harm if they are stolen. But for your banking or financial information sites and similar applications, create very secure passwords and use a different one for each site or account.

Change Passwords Often

The longer you use a password the longer people have to steal it or figure it out. When they do manage to figure it out they will continue to use it as long as it remains valid.

To further limit the damage change your passwords at least once a year and perhaps two or three times a year on your really important accounts.

When you replace your passwords do not make them similar such as just adding one character or changing a number from 1 to 2 or something like that. Make them completely different so the hackers do not have a head start on figuring out your new passwords.

Shred Documents

We all get statements and notices with account and personal information on them. Do NOT throw these in the garbage without shredding them first. Going through the garbage is one well know way people get private information from people.

Shredders are not expensive and you don't need a professional model. Just get one that can shred paper and credit cards so you can shred those as well when they expire. Remember that those have account numbers on them that do not change when the cards are renewed. An option to shredding might be to burn them in your fireplace or fire bit. You could consider that another form of recycling. Do not burn credit cards as they will just melt and make a mess.

Screen Phone Calls & Requests Carefully

Any time you get a call asking you to verify your personal information, do not provide it.

These are well known ways for scammers to get you to tell them your personal information. Instead, call the company back on a number that YOU find for them in the phone book or on your statement.

Do NOT use a call back number the caller provides as you have no idea where that number really is going. Of course, if you can go to the company in person to provide the information or to check to make sure the request was valid that is the best option. Remember any time you give information over the phone you don't know who is listening on the other end of the phone or whether or not there are any devices on the phone line. NEVER give someone your password over the phone or change it over the phone!

Do Not Respond to E-mails Asking to Update or Provide Personal Information

This just might be the number one way that people get other people's information today. E-mails or websites designed to look EXACTLY like the real website ask you to provide or verify your information for some security based reason. Then you enter your information to "verify" it and BOOM! They got your private information.

These are usually very good looking and well written e-mails. Some will say that it is time for you to change your password. Then they ask you for your current password before you can change it and they log that password into their system and they have your login information.

Follow the same procedure whenever you get one of these e-mails. Go directly to the company either in person or on a number that you know is the right one and ask them if the request is legitimate. If it is follow their instructions.

If you are asked legitimately to change a password, you can change it online but after you do, go back to the main website and check the new login information. If it works with the new password you are probably OK. But if it doesn't work but still works with your old password, you might have been hacked. Call the company immediately to report this.

Check Credit Reports Yearly

We have said it before and we will say it again. Review your credit report at least once a year to make sure there are no strange entries and no new accounts that you personally did not agree to or open. Sometimes this is the only way you will find out if someone has opened an account in your name.

The faster you find out the better the chance of limiting the damage done to your credit score or rating.

Notify Others When you are Hacked

If you ever find yourself being hacked or your information stolen by anyone, notify the company involved immediately to report it.

Sometimes a company server will be hacked and the only way they might be aware of it is if someone else reports the problem to them.

You should also report it so that they can suspend your current account so that further damage is not done and then issue you a new card. Since identity theft is something that almost every card is protected against, you should not have to pay for unauthorized charges once you notify them. But if your bank account has been hacked and money taken out, you might have a tough time getting it back.

How to Save Money

While having a great credit rating and a high credit score is wonderful, we still need to save money. Because you cannot live solely on credit even if you wanted to. You might be able to live on it for now, but eventually it will catch up to you and you will have to rely on your savings and overall financial portfolio.

So at this point we want to give you some tips, tools and ideas to help you not only get back on your feet credit-wise but also help you save money for your near and long-term future. Here are a few things you should be aware of when it comes to financial planning and saving money:

What the True Value of Money Represents

I know people who say they don't need much to be happy. And truthfully they really don't. They appear happy without luxury cars or fancy vacations and they have a nice house without needing it to be huge and expensive.

So you might draw a conclusion from this that these people don't need much money.

And you wouldn't be more wrong.

Money is not just about buying things or going places or living extravagant lifestyles. Having money is not about having possessions. It is all about having options. You see money allows you the options to do more of what you want and to do more things the way you want to do them.

For example, if you have enough money, you can retire where you want to instead of where they tell you. You can have the quality of medical care that you can afford rather than the type of care you qualify for. You can get the treatment you need rather than the treatment you can afford.

Most people get so hung up on buying things and having things that they lose focus on what money really means to us throughout our lives. Having more options and choices is almost always the better way to do. As we have said earlier in this book the world is full of people who complain they don't have enough money. But there are very few people who complain that they have too much.

You might not need a fortune but you are going to need some. So as we go through the next few pages keep this in mind. You want to have the money to be able to live life as you see it not as someone else determines it should be for you.

The Earlier the Better

When it comes to saving money, there are two very important things you should always remember. They are related to each other and they have to do with timing.

The first thing to remember is to start as early as you can. Don't put it off until tomorrow or next month or next year. Start now. The earlier you start, the more money you will have and the faster you will get where you want to be.

The second thing to remember is that if you don't start right now, or if you have been putting this off for quite a while, it is never too late to start saving. You won't have as much money as if you started earlier although if you save more each year you still can recover. But there is no better time to start than right now whether you are 20 or 60 years old. Start right now to get the best result!

Even a Little is Better than Nothing at All

Some people think that they have to contribute huge amounts of money to make a difference in their lives. The fact is, the more money you save the better off you will be but no matter what you save it will still be better than nothing.

Even the longest marathon starts off with a single step and taking that step, no matter how small will get you that much closer to your goal.

If you never save even a dime you will never have even a dime. So whether you can save 10 cents or $10,000 the most important thing is to start the saving process and let things take over from there!

The Power of Compound Interest

Here is the one most important reason to start saving as early as you can. Compound interest is a wonderful thing. Not only do you get interest on what you saved but the next year you get interest not only on what you saved but on the interest that your money earned over the last year! So your money builds faster and faster as the interest earned gets larger and larger.

So the earlier you start saving the longer that money will sit there and earn interest upon interest upon interest. You will be astounded on how far you money can take you if you only give it time to really get working for you!

Creating a Cushion

Everyone needs a cushion of money to get them through tough times and unexpected expenses.

We talked about this earlier in the book but it must be part of everyone's long term financial portfolio anyway.

When you have saved your own money it is there whenever you need it. You don't have to worry about whether it will be there or if it can be taken away from you at any point in time. Having a cushion of money in the bank allows you the ultimate flexibility to be able to do what you want when you want and the way you want.

As we said the experts recommend 6 months of liquid assets. This might be too much for a lot of people but the bottom line should be to have enough money in easily available resources to tide you over until you can transfer assets from other sources. So if the bulk of you money is in stocks and it will take you 30 days to get those funds when you need them, have at least 5 weeks' worth of liquid assets to hold you through that time.

This will help you avoid having to go the credit route and pay the higher interest rates on the funds you will need. In turn this will help you maintain a higher credit rating by showing more responsibly use of your available credit. This is just one small piece of your overall financial planning.

Long-Term vs. Short-Term Views

Depending on how old we are, we must think about both our long-term and short-term financial goals.

By that I means how much money we are going to need over the next few years to do what we need to do and then how much money we are going to need long-term for such things as our retirement and our children's education, e=wedding and other things.

We must remember that life doesn't take care of itself. We have to plan things out to a certain extent so that we are prepared for things when they come along. We cannot wait until our sons and daughter send out college application to start saving for college. This must be done 10 or 15 years earlier to allow our savings and compound interest to help us meet our goals.

So many people live paycheck to paycheck and think only about today. They spend money as fast as they can make it and give no thought to what they might need tomorrow. Then tomorrow rolls around and they have no money for retirement, their kids are up to the butts in student loans and their kids wedding reception is held at the local McDonalds!

So do yourselves a favor and work out a rough plan for what is likely going to come up over the rest of your financial life. Think not only about today but give some thought to all the tomorrows ahead.

Otherwise those tomorrows are going to be a lot different than you pictured they would be.

Retirement Savings

If you really want a wake-up call, consider this mind-blowing statistic: Approximately half the people who retire today or within a few years will not have saved anything towards their retirement! That means those people are going to walk into retirement being almost totally dependent on Social Security. Many of those people have no pensions either as pensions are rapidly becoming a thing of the past!

With the average Social Security payment being less than $2,000 a month, these people are going to find it very difficult to support themselves in their retirement! The bottom line is that if you are going to lead a fairly happy and mostly stress free retirement, you are going to have to start saving for it and planning for it early!

We are not retirement experts and do not pretend to be so we will leave it at this:

There are many options for people when it comes to retirement savings. We have company sponsored plans like 401K, 403B and other accounts. We also have personal or private options such as regular IRA's, Roth IRA's and other options.

All of these have different investment choices and different tax impacts and exemptions. We strongly suggest that you contact a financial advisor or retirement investment company to discuss your best options. There are a lot of things to consider and you should always talk to someone before making your decision.

But regardless of which investment option you choose, the best overall approach is the same. Start early and invest as much as you can afford. Over time you will create a larger overall investment portfolio and be able to retire with more savings and more options.

Do not think that retirement is so far off you don't have to do anything now. In fact, the exact opposite is true. With the power of compound interest, the money you save earliest will often have the greatest overall impact. Though you can recover by saving more later, compound interest allows you to gather a larger savings level with less overall sacrifice.

Company Retirement Plans

If you are fortunate to have a company sponsored retirement plan with a company matching benefit, then you have an opportunity that you would be a fool not to take advantage of. Company matching is a benefit where the company will match your contributions at a certain rate up to a certain dollar figure.

Sometimes this is a specific percentage of your salary and other times it is specified as dollars and cents.

Regardless of how much they match this is like getting money for nothing. You should always contribute at least up to the level that the company matches.

So if the company matches the first 5% of your salary if you contribute the same then you should contribute at least 5%. You can contribute more even though the company won't match it but that first 5% is what really matters.

This is like receiving an extra 5% of your salary as a reward for you saving for your retirement. You save 5%, the company gives you 5% so you are saving double the amount it is costing you and getting FREE money! Plus, it is all coming out before taxes so that 5% you are contributing is costing you even less.

While I understand that you might have other debt to pay down, the company matching rate usually makes this a no brainer to do despite your other debt. If there is any doubt, or if you really think you might do better elsewhere, PLEASE check with a financial advisor before you pass up this potential windfall!

Pay Yourself First

We can always seem to find other things to spend our money on so there is nothing left at the end of the month for us to save. This is because we put our expenses first and our savings last. As contrary or foolish as this might seem, we need to pay ourselves first before we take care of our bills and expenses.

For example, if we take home $2,000 a month but we take off $200 before we do our budget and earmark that money towards savings, then our budget will reflect a take home pay of $1,800. We design our budget around that figure and we then pay our bills and figure out our expenses based on that figure. The end result is that we automatically save that $200 a month without having to do anything. If we can use payroll deduction to take that $200 out automatically for us we will never even see that money or really miss it.

Now this all assumes that after we take out that $200, or however much we decide, that we will still have enough left over to pay our bills and expenses. If we save money and that causes us to go into debt and pay 18% or more for our credit then that will usually defeat the purpose. But if we can take the money out first and still pay our expenses, this is the best and easiest way to save money for the future or other reasons.

Taking this approach eliminates us looking at our bank balance at the end of the month and seeing that surplus deciding to buy a new TV or other product because we have the money. Buying stuff is always more fun and attractive than saving that money in the bank. A lot of people are able to resist the temptation but some are not.

The other benefit is that when we pay ourselves first we will stand a much better chance of making that payment first.

It is even better when we use an automatic deduction. It takes us totally out of the process. If we do this manually every month after paying expenses if we miss just one deposit for one month we are behind the game. And once we miss one payment something else in our brains will tell us that is no big deal and we can miss another or a few more.

Do yourself a favor and pay yourself first before you creditors and other expenses.

Payroll Deduction

Sometimes the best savings plans are the plans that do the saving for us. If your employer offers the ability to send direct deposit transfers to outside financial institutions then this might be the ideal way for you to force yourself to save money.

Using direct deposit you can designate regular scheduled transfers from your employer direct to your bank, credit union or other savings organization. This way you never even see the money and you do not have to do a manual transfer every month. Whenever you have to do these transfers manually you run the risk of forgetting or not making them because you want to use the money in another way.

If you cannot make these transfers direct through your employer then another option is to set up direct transfers from your checking account directly into savings. This is the next best thing as you just have to remember to deduct the amount from your bank balance so you can keep your checking balance accurate.

But be aware that you will still "see" this money every month as you make note of the transfer. So you will be reminded every month of the transfer. If you can keep the transfer going every month and not be tempted to stop it for any reason, this can still work out very well for you.

Banking the Raise

Here is another way to not "feel" the loss of money coming out of your bank account for savings. The next time you get a salary increase, figure out the difference you will have in your paycheck and do some kind of direct transfer of that money into a savings account.

This way you can save money while still having the same amount in your bank account every month to use to pay bills.

This is also a great way to save for retirement as well. The only difference is that you can take the full amount of the raise and increase your retirement contributions by the same amount because those funds will be taken out pre-tax. So you get to save more money in that manner than if you were saving it for any other reason.

But we should always remind you that there needs to always be a balance between saving for retirement and saving for today. Because of the large penalties for early withdrawal from retirement accounts, money that is saved for retirement should not be withdrawn until you reach or exceed the minimum retirement age.

Think Balanced

While savings of any kind are always useful, we should develop an overall balanced plan of savings that addresses both the needs of today with the needs of tomorrow as well. That means making sure we are prepared for both long-term and short-term needs.

One thing to remember is that money saved for today that is not used for its intended purpose will still be able to grow over time and will be available for the future as well. That means your short-term savings can also be used for your long-term needs as well. So it is not like you will be losing or wasting funds that you designate for short-term use that wind up not being needed.

So the question at this time usually is "How do I determine which type of savings I need at this time in my life?"

Well, the answer is not as simple as one might think. Everyone's situation is different and therefore we all will have different levels and types of needs.

People with children, for example, will need more money than single people or couples with no children. Their expenses will be higher, they will have college to plan and save for and they will still have their retirement and later years to think about as well. The married couple with no children will just themselves to think about and their savings portfolio will look different because their needs are different.

Personally, I believe that everyone should at least have a consultation with an investment and retirement advisor at different stages in their lives. Depending on your age and individual situation that might mean every 10 years or every 5 years.

During this consultation you can re-evaluate your current and future needs, your planned expenses and your current financial debt and other obligations.

This is useful because as your life changes so do your needs and your investments should change with them.

Though there is a cost for these consultations, you will find that your peace of mind and the overall performance of your investments will usually make this cost well worthwhile.

Overall Positive &

Responsible Attitudes

The last chapter of this book is going to deal with your attitudes towards personal finance, credit and how they apply in your life. This chapter will explore a few of the mindsets that responsible people should have as they go through life. You might agree or disagree with each one and that doesn't necessarily mean that either of us are wrong.

All it does mean is that everyone is different and everyone has their own ideas of how people should go through life. But sometimes it is good to hear opposing views in case you were not made aware of certain things as you went through life. No matter how old we get, or how much education we have received along the way, there are always new things to be learned and new knowledge to implement.

Hopefully here you will find some of that new knowledge:

Be Responsible

Look, we all go through life and hopefully look at things with some kind of moral and ethical filter. In other words, we look at things and determine whether they are right or wrong. Most of us have pretty similar filter when it comes to right and wrong.

But we also need another filter and that is one that looks at things from the point of view of whether or not what we are thinking about doing is responsible or not. The problem is that far too many people today do whatever they want whether or not it is the responsible thing to do.

Part of being an adult is being able to set impulse aside and do what's right. So if you are thinking about buying things you want but can't afford, the adult part of you should be telling you that this is not the responsibly thing to do. The "little kind inside" might be screaming that they want something but the responsible adult side has to say no. That does not happen nearly as often as it needs to.

Most of us get that funny feeling when we start doing something that part of us feels is wrong or irresponsible. Whenever we have that feeling we shouldn't ignore it. Instead, we should stop and figure out why we feel that way. If we listen to those little voices inside us and do what is responsible, we would all be better off.

Another part of this is that we should be taking responsibility for everything we do.

We should take credit for the good decisions and take the blame for the bad ones as well. Because when we take responsibility and don't blame others, we tend to learn more and make fewer mistakes. The only thing wrong with making a mistake is making the same mistake twice or three times because you didn't learn anything the first time.

So moving forward, think things through and do what is best for you long-term instead of what might feel good or look good in the moment. If everyone handled their personal finances and credit in this manner we would have far fewer bankruptcies.

Don't Rely on Others or Anything

I often find it puzzling to hear how some people place alt office or program. While it is all right to use those services and programs as part of your financial planning, you would be foolish to place all your faith in the premise that someone is always going to be there to bail you out of whatever problem you might get yourself into.

I also would not place my face in believing that someone is always going to be there to help you either. While this might sound cynical, even the best and most trustworthy and reliable people are not going to be around forever so don't put your future in the hands of anyone but yourself.

Ask for help when you need it, follow the instructions of those far more knowledgeable than you are and learn what you need to know about making responsible decisions. But let those decisions be yours and do not allow other's to make decisions for you. They can advise, they can educate and they can recommend. But only YOU should be in charge of your future.

You can plan to live on Social Security and not save anything but what happens if Social Security should go away or reduce the benefits? Will your future go up in flames because you decided it was better for others to take care of you? Or will you have made your own plans to add to your security?

It is always better to be self-sufficient and self-sustaining instead of hoping that someone or some government program will still be around when you need it. Take back control of your financial planning and future and take it back now!

Live Within Your Means

There are some things in this world that shouldn't have to be said. These are just the common sense parts of life that everyone should understand. But evidently these things are lost on some people so we have to cover them anyway.

One of these common sense approaches should be that we should all live within our means.

That means not spending more than we earn, not buying things we cannot afford and not attempting to live a lifestyle that requires more resources than we can ever hope to have.

This means not purchasing a 12 bedroom house when all you can afford is a 3 bedroom ranch. It means not purchasing a Mercedes when all you can afford is a used Chevrolet. So many people have found themselves in so much trouble because they tried to live above their means.

It also means not falling victim to the entitlement virus. You are entitled to live your life free of persecution and prejudice. You are not entitled to Hawaii vacations, fancy cars, designer handbags and a summer home on the water. If you want those things you are going to have to educate yourself and work for them.

It is amazing how many people have found themselves so deeply in debt because they thought they deserved what their neighbors had. The only problem is that they didn't want to put in the time and effort those neighbors did in order to afford those things.

Think Twice, Purchase Once

A large part of our credit problems have come about because we just make it too damned easy to buy stuff today.

Internet shopping, one click purchasing, stored credit card information and all other things that make it so easy and so painless to purchase means that it is just too easy to spend money these days.

It used to be that you saw something in the store and you then had to go to the bank, withdraw the money and go back to make the purchase. But somewhere during that process you had second thoughts and decided you really didn't need that deluxe left handed cheese straighter you saw in the store and you didn't buy it.

Today impulse buys are so easy we wind up with far too many things we do not need or that we paid too much for and all we have are closets full of crap and a large credit card bill. Instead of that, we should adopt a policy of think twice and buy later.

Give some of your purchases the gift of time. Don't buy them today. Give yourself a day or so to really think about it. Then, if you still really want the products, go back and buy them. You will probably find yourself with far less junk, more room in your closets and much smaller credit card bills with much lower finance charges.

But Quality, Not Price

Sometimes in our attempts to save money we wind up spending even more.

A prime example is when we try to save a few pennies by buying a cheaper version of the product we need. While this might work if it is something we use infrequently or just one or two times, we are almost far better off purchasing a quality item once or twice than purchasing the cheaper version 6 or 8 times.

I have tools that I have been using for 40 years and they still work perfectly. That is because they are quality tools that I paid a good price for. But I have had other tools and equipment that were not high quality that failed after a few years and then had to be purchased again.

Do yourself a favor and do not buy because of price alone. Research the quality and reputation of the brand and factor that into your decision. Far too much money has been wasted paying good money for really crappy products that just don't last.

Insure Yourself Responsibly

Last but not least, no book on credit or finances would be complete without at least mentioning insurance. That is because insurance almost has to be part of your overall financial plan especially if you are married or have a family.

While it would be wonderful to say that everyone needs a certain amount of insurance of this type and that type that is certainly not the case.

Everyone is different and everyone has different needs and different situations. So you need to figure out what is best for you.

The problem is that no one is really sure who to go to for this type of information. Insurance agents sell insurance by commission so they have their own interests in getting you to buy as much insurance as you can possibly afford. The more you purchase the more they get paid. So asking an insurance agent if you should purchase insurance is asking the clerk at McDonald's if they think you should get fries with your burger. Of course they are going to say you should!

Generally speaking, if you are responsible for the support of other family members, you should make sure you are insured sufficiently so that if you should pass away they would have their needs met until the point where they could provide for themselves.

If you have a mortgage you might want to have insurance that would pay off the house should you pass away while your spouse was still alive. This way they would not lose the house if you passed on.

There are so many type of insurance and so many different situations and reasons you almost need to find an accountant or financial advisor to help you navigate through the tons of different types of insurance and coverages.

Insurance is important but over insuring yourself just might be nothing more than a waste of money that will ultimately benefit someone else a lot more than it benefitted you.

Conclusion

It is my hope that you now have a broader understanding or credit and personal finance than you had prior to opening this book. They say knowledge is money and they are 100% correct. Knowledge is also power as it gives you the power to make the right decisions and take the right steps as you go through life.

If you are currently in financial trouble I am confident that you can dig your way out of it if you learn how to be financially responsible. There are so many resources out there to help you that everyone should be able to recover. It just takes time.

But it also takes commitment and it also takes strength. It takes strength to admit that some of what you were doing just wasn't working and that you understand that. It also takes the strength to undergo change and to stick with those changes for as long as they are needed. But the good news is that most of us have that strength. We just lack the ability to focus it properly.

If I were to have one last bit of advice it would be this:

Go through life the right way. Don't take short cuts with your finances or let other make your financial decisions for you. If you need help get the right help. Stay away from those who claim they can solve all your credit problems in 15 minutes because they just can't do that.

Take the high road and rehabilitate your credit the right way. Chanel your efforts in the right directions that will give you the results you need for not only the next few weeks or months but for the next few years. There might be times in your life when you can take a shortcut. But trust me when I say that this is most certainly not one of them.

If you are going to hire outside help, check them out thoroughly. A commercial on television or an ad in the Yellow Pages is not an endorsement. Outlandish claims that appear to be too good to be true are usually not true at all. Do your research. Check people out and make responsible decisions.

Remember that even though people may advise you and counsel you, when you sign your name on a form that makes YOU the one they will come after if and when something goes wrong. You cannot plead ignorance and you cannot plead stupidity either. Once you sign something, you own it.

Take your time, make the right choices and do the right thing. That will greatly increase the odds that you will get to where you want to be with the fewest set-backs and bumps in the road.

Good Luck!

Resource Page

Contact Information for Major Credit Reporting Companies

Equifax: 1-800-525-6285
www.equifax.com

Experian :   1-888-397-3742
www.experian.com

Transunion: 1-800-680-7289
www.transunion.com

For a FREE copy of your credit reports, please go to:
www.annualcreditreport.com

For free credit scores:
www.creditkarma.com

For more information on Identity Theft, go to:
ftc.gov/idtheft

For more information on credit repair scams, please go to:
Consumer.ftc.gov

For more information on credit building, financial planning and other life planning events, please sign up for our financial newsletter available at:

http://www.26ways.com/financial.htm

The newsletter is free, there is no obligation and we will never rent. Share or sell your information to anyone for any reason. We hate it when someone does that to us so we sure aren't going to do it to you!

www.ingramcontent.com/pod-product-compliance
Lightning Source LLC
Chambersburg PA
CBHW051917170526
45168CB00001B/428